The Curriculum Manager's Handbook

Defining the Job of a Curriculum Manager in Performance Competence Terms

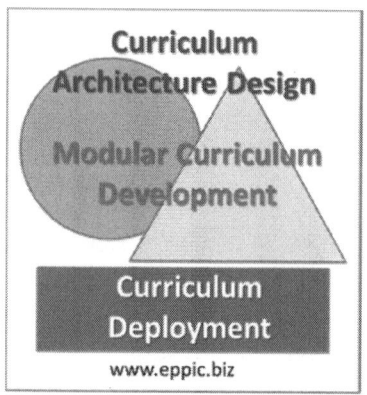

Guy W. Wallace

The Wallace 6-Pack
for Instructional Systems Design for an Enterprise Context
- Paperback and Kindle -

1. **The Curriculum Manager's Handbook**
2. **Analysis of Performance Competence Requirements**
3. **Performance-Based Curriculum Architecture Design**
4. **Performance-Based Modular Curriculum Development**
5. **Developing Your Management Areas of Performance Competence**
6. **From Training to Performance Improvement Consulting**

- **Guy W. Wallace Books For Sale** new in 2011 -
See the Resources Tab at: **www.eppic.biz**

The Curriculum Manager's Handbook

Copyright © 2011 Guy W. Wallace

All rights reserved.

ISBN-10: 146355558X
ISBN-13: 978-1463555580

To order additional copies of this book please go to the Resources Tab at:

www.eppic.biz

DEDICATION

To my wife Nancy – thank you for everything! You make all things possible!

CONTENTS

	Acknowledgments	i
1	What Does a Curriculum Manager Do?	1
2	AoP: Stakeholder Needs Assessment & Alignment	27
3	AoP: Strategic Planning & Management	53
4	AoP: Operations Planning & Management	65
5	AoP: Results Measurement	79
6	AoP: Improvement Planning	95
7	AoP: Communications	107
8	AoP: Product & Service Line Design	120
9	AoP: Product & Service Line Development	143
10	AoP: Product & Service Line Deployment	169
11	AoP: Process Design & Redesign	193
12	AoP: Human Assets	203
13	AoP: Environmental Assets	222
14	AoP: Special Assignments	241
15	Summary & Close	247
16	Additional Related Resources & References	254

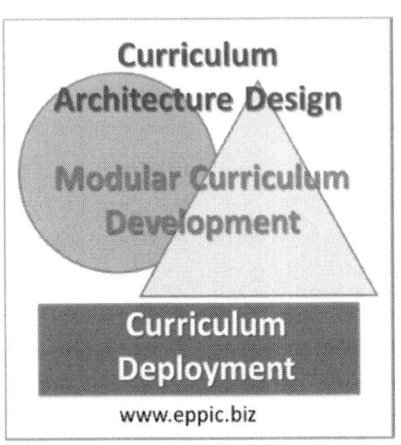

At the Core of a Curriculum Manager's
Performance Competence Requirements
are the architecture, development and deployment of
performance-enabling
Instructional and Informational Content

ACKNOWLEDGMENTS

To my many clients over the past three decades – each of whom has taught me much about meeting their unique needs and constraints in improving performance competence of their key Target Audiences – for the sake of the business, by design.

And to my professional colleagues and friends at ISPI, the International Society for Performance Improvement – I owe so much to so many of you! Thank you all for sharing so much all of these past 3 decades of my involvement!

Learning & Development for the Sake of the Enterprise.

1 – WHAT DOES A CURRICULUM MANAGER DO?

Chapter Overview

This chapter is intended to provide you with an extensive overview of the flexible model that we will use to enable you to adapt and define your specific role as a Curriculum Manager in your context so that you might perform your job assignment competently.

Book Overview

What a Curriculum Manager actually does varies from one Enterprise to the next – and perhaps even differently within any one Enterprise as well. Even the job title of Curriculum Manager is likely to be different.

Sometimes the job is simply titled: Training Manager, or Learning Manager. Sometimes it is: Learning &

Development Manager. Some jobs might be titled: Learning Architect. Others: Chief Learning Officer, or CLO.

So what does a Curriculum Manager, by any job title, do?

What are their Performance Competence requirements?

Are they the same from job to job despite all the variation in titles?

No. There is variation in both job titles and in job expectations.

This book intends to provide you with a model that you can use to define your job as a Curriculum Manager for your specific context – for your Enterprise.

And your adaptation of this model will be dependent on all of the other expectations for all of the other managers and individual contributor jobs in your Training, Learning and Knowledge Management organization – and what's expected of them.

Therefore some of what will be covered in this book will be others' roles and responsibilities.

Given all of the variation that exists in the jobs titled Curriculum Manager – or something akin to that – our broad definition is this:

A Curriculum Manager is responsible for addressing the performance-based learning needs and performance support needs of targeted Learners/Performers, as identified and prioritized by their internal Customers and Stakeholders.

Success is probably measured based on the ability of the Curriculum Manager to provide of performance-required, authentic content, before and/or during the moment of need, that positively impacts performance on-the-job both effectively and efficiently.

Content of any blend; any media and mode that is appropriate. How you accomplish that is key.

Content can be of any deployment mode that is appropriate to both the needs and constraints of the Learners and their management. Learners are Performers first – and who perform within an Enterprise Performance Context. They are Learners second – who Learn in an Enterprise Learning Context. It is not "all about Learning" – it is "all about Performance."

Focus on Performance – and enable that.

Included in the blend of modes for Training, Learning and Knowledge Management can be any of the following, but they are certainly not limited to:

- Instructor-led Training

- E-Learning
- Webinars
- Coached/Mentored Learning
- Task Assignments
- Job Assignments
- Books, chapters and article reading assignments
- Guided Self-Discovery Learning by any means

Curriculum – a somewhat old fashioned term – is a set of Instructional and Informational Content that is as Rigorous as Required and as Flexible as Feasible.

The following are *generalizations*, meaning that they are mostly right and sometimes wrong…

- The newer the Performer is to the job the more guidance, the more formal the learning should be. They simply don't know what they don't know and need to know.

- The more experienced the Performer is the less formal their learning requirements may be and the less guidance they need.

And we are concerned here with an **Enterprise Learning Context** – versus an Educational Learning Context or a Personal Learning Context.

As a good steward of shareholder equity, the Curriculum Manager effectively and efficiently enables performance back on-the-job for their Targeted Audiences through a variety of means. Some of that happens in more traditional ways; and some happens in newer, non-traditional ways.

As always, it depends. It depends on the context. Which is always somewhat unique.

You will most likely need to adapt the model presented in this book – if it is inappropriate to merely adopt. And it is probably inappropriate for you to merely adopt what I am presenting here.

Every Enterprise Training, Learning and Knowledge Management function is organized differently at some level – and you will need to first determine what could be adopted, and what will need to be adapted – and then do so.

Speaking of adaptations, you may need to start here, your own adaptation of my adaptation of the phrase "Training, Learning and Knowledge Management" which I have converted to L&D and to T&D.

Throughout the rest of this book I will refer to what is often labeled something along the lines of "Training, Learning and Knowledge Management" as L&D – for: Learning & Development and T&D – for: Training & Development. They are both equivalent in my use throughout this book.

By L&D or T&D I mean the *performance-based* instruction and/or information required to enable performance – some of which must be learned prior to the moment of need – and then available via recall during the moment of need. And some may simply be available for reference during the moment of need. And sometimes content is handled both ways.

L&D in the context of this book creates the necessary awareness, knowledge and/ or skill needed by a Target Audience of the Curriculum Manager.

That in fact is the core of the Curriculum Manager's job: provisioning the right L&D content, instructional and/or informational, to the Target Audience in the right amount, at the right time, with the right quality to enable that Target Audiences' Performance Competence.

The model that we will use to define the Curriculum Manager's job is itself an adaptation of "The Management Areas of Performance Model."

The Management Areas of Performance model or framework was derived in the 1990s from over 20 analyses of management and leadership performance by this author and his former business partners – and then used and validated in over 15 follow-on analyses of management and leadership performance by me; as well as by additional applications by my clients and their staff after either the formal or informal development of those staff members in my analysis methods by me.

After an overview of this model in this first chapter we will dive in and explore the typical outputs, tasks and process details and in the succeeding chapters.

You will be asked to reflect on the chapter content and think about your adaptation requirements at the conclusion of each chapter before proceeding to the next chapter, or whichever chapter you decide is the most logical for your context and needs.

The books wraps up with a fairly short list of additional resources and references – all directly related to what was covered in this book; and most written or co-written by this author.

There are of course, hundreds or thousands of related resources. Rather than overwhelm you with those almost limitless opportunities to explore further – I have narrowed my suggested reading list to those offering more details on what I am presenting here.

Let's begin.

The Curriculum Manager's Areas of Performance Competence Model

This model creates a work breakdown structure of a Curriculum Manager's job responsibilities. It includes three "tiers" or levels to organize the Performance Competence Requirements for this Target Audience, the Curriculum Manager – or whatever title this role is given in your Enterprise.

Those three tiers are:

- Leadership
- Core
- Support

The following graphic presents those three tiers with additional responsibility areas – otherwise known as Areas of Performance.

Curriculum Manager's Areas of Performance Competence Model

LEADERSHIP AoPs - Planning & Management
- ❏ Stakeholder Needs Assessment & Alignment
- ❏ Strategic Planning
- ❏ Operations Planning
- ❏ Results Measurement
- ❏ Improvement Planning
- ❏ Communications

CORE AoPs - Planning & Management
- ❏ Product & Service Line Design
- ❏ Product & Service Line Development
- ❏ Product & Service Line Deployment

SUPPORT AoPs - Planning & Management
- ❏ Process Design and Redesign
- ❏ Human Assets
- ❏ Environmental Assets
- ❏ Special Assignments

Adapted from the Management Areas of Performance Model
©2002 Guy W. Wallace

There are 13 Areas of Performance (AoPs) in total in this adapted model – and we will cover each one in the chapters of this book – for you to adapt to your needs to define your job in your context.

First lets quickly overview each of the 13 AoPs and then look at them again within the context of our three tiered model.

The 13 are:

- AoP: **Stakeholder Needs Assessment & Alignment**. This is the most critical aspect of your role – getting aligned to the priorities of your Customers and other Stakeholders. This can be done formally – or informally.

- AoP: **Strategic Planning & Management**. Getting yourself and your organization ready for the future while attending to the present may be tricky – but it is necessary. Document these so that you can share them in your collaboration with your Customers and Stakeholders.

- AoP: **Operations Planning & Management**. Getting a handle on your plans and budgets for the current year is necessary if you hope to actually achieve the goals and plans everyone else has for you. Document these so that you can share them in your collaboration with your Customers and Stakeholders.

- AoP: **Results Measurement**. Measure and report out what is important to your Customers and Stakeholders using their business metrics, not just Learning Metrics.

- AoP: **Improvement Planning**. Plan to improve where it makes sense and makes you more effective and efficient a Steward of shareholder equity.

- AoP: **Communications**. This is where you would plan for both proactive and reactive communications for some or all of your key Stakeholders.

- AoP: **Product & Service Line Design**. This is where both a Portfolio Plan and a Curriculum Architecture Design is done for the most critical of your Target Audiences.

- AoP: **Product & Service Line Development**. This is where you use an ADDIE-like approach to new product (and service) development.

- AoP: **Product & Service Line Deployment**. This is where you deliberately look at the systems you have in place to deploy – and/or make accessible – your products and services.

- AoP: **Process Design & Redesign**. This is where you document existing processes, create new ones, or improve old ones that need it (but only if there is enough R for the I).

- AoP: **Human Assets**. This is where you put all of the human resources (assets) into place to bring your paper processes to life.

- AoP: **Environmental Assets**. This is where you put everything else in place to assist your human resources (assets) in bringing your paper processes to life.

- AoP: **Special Assignments**. This is a catch all – but it would be good for you to have documented these "other duties" as they may be hindering your effectiveness in your Curriculum Manager role.

If these 13 Areas of Performance make sense to you as being part of your job as a Curriculum Manager, then this book is for you!

Now let's review the three tiers of our model more closely.

The Leadership Areas of Performance Competence

These Areas of Performance are all about you, the Curriculum Manager, figuring out what is needed from you and your team now and in the future given your Customers and Stakeholders' requirements and constraints, and then dealing with the resources available to you to get those expectations met. You also will be measuring and reporting results, making improvements to your own systems and processes, and proactively and reactively providing general and specific communications to all of the appropriate constituencies you are responsible for serving.

This includes the following six **Leadership AoPs**:

1. Stakeholder Needs Assessment & Alignment
2. Strategic Planning
3. Operations Planning
4. Results Measurement
5. Improvement Planning
6. Communications

Let's now look a little deeper at each of the AoPs in level 1 – the **Leadership** tier – of the model.

> **L1- Stakeholder Needs Assessment & Alignment** is about the data gathering regarding all Stakeholders' needs, including but beyond your immediate Customers: the Learners and their management. This is gathering feedback on how well your products and services are doing – from their perspectives – in

meeting those needs currently, and their thoughts about your likely readiness to serve their future needs.

Once all of these Stakeholders' needs and wants are better understood, your goals can be established and aligned, appropriate to any balancing of any Stakeholder Requirement conflicts that may exist.

And - just because you can define a valid need for Instruction – does not warrant meeting that need. Not if there are resource constraints – and when aren't there? This should be clear to your collective Customer and Stakeholders – or you can never win.

L2- Strategic Planning is about the setting of your longer-term strategic goals based on and aligned to those of your Customers and Stakeholders. Then you document your plans to achieve those Stakeholder Requirements – so that that might be reviewed and approved and sanctioned by those Stakeholders.

If you are not planning on doing enough – in their eyes – and that's due to your resource constraints – then this is the way to remedy that – if possible. They hold the purse strings – so to speak. They live with the consequences of you not being ready and able to meet their needs in the future.

L3- Operations Planning addresses the development and management of your operational (annual) plan to achieve the assigned year's annual goals/objectives along with the longer-term strategic goals and plans. There are things you may need to do now, early in order to be ready later.

Again, if you are not planning on doing enough – in their eyes – and that's due to your resource constraints – then this is the way to remedy that – if possible.

L4- Results Measurement focuses on the establishment of a meaningful scorecard set of measures – and putting the measurement mechanisms for the gathering and reporting in place. There is relevant data and information required by each of your Stakeholders – those that are related to and aligned with their desired Enterprise results – not your 4 or 5 levels of Learning Metrics.

Those Learning Metrics are important – but those are measures and results for you – your Stakeholders. They care about business metrics; "frankly they don't give a damn my dear" (paraphrasing from Gone With the Wind) about the 4 or 5 levels you might do for your own diagnostics efforts – except for that final Learning metric – Results or ROI.

By the way: when I learned the 4 level version of this model in 1979 I was taught that Results were always ROI. So my bias has always been away from measurements of Learning toward measurements of Performance using business metrics.

L5- Improvement Planning is about the systematic improvement of internal processes and/or their human and environmental asset provisioning systems within your control as a Curriculum Manager – and they are done exclusively for ROI benefit, and to achieve your annual and long-term (strategic) goals and plans – and your immediate operational plans.

Again, as these are aligned with your Stakeholders' needs and constraints – they should see value in you doing these for yourself in terms of what it does for them.

L6- Communications addresses the planning and management of both proactive and reactive communications.

You as a Curriculum Manager may have many Stakeholders – and perhaps you need to communicate formally, routinely with each and every constituency – and perhaps not.

Being deliberate about which Community constituency you will attend to – and how – is what this Area of Performance is all about.

In fact – that is what all of these AoPs are about: determining which you will focus on deliberately as part of your role as a Curriculum Manager – by any job title!

Content Context Check

- Does the role of Curriculum Manager in your Enterprise include these Leadership responsibilities?

- If they do not, should they?

- Are they currently the responsibility of some other job – and if so, is that working well enough?

Leadership AoPs Overview Summary

All of these Leadership AoPs are **not** about leading and managing **in the moment**, – but are about leadership and management activities focused more on both the long-term and medium-term performance of you and your team in meeting the needs of your Customers and Stakeholders, of your overall Enterprise, as driven by or limited by the current context of your industry and the current situation it is in – its current position in the business cycle.

The **Planning & Management** aspect of these Leadership Areas of Performance includes:

> **Planning the Work** – which is about deciding what gets done and by whom and when.
>
> **Assigning the Work** – which addresses the communications of the work assignment.
>
> **Monitoring the Work** – which focuses on the follow up monitoring of work processes and/or work products to insure that everything is okay.
>
> **Troubleshooting the Work** – which addresses the following up on any work product or process discrepancies to resolve them.

These six **Leadership AoPs** of a Curriculum Manager will be covered in greater detail in chapters 2 – 7.

You will do your thinking about any specific adaptations that you might need for your context when reading those chapters.

Next we move to the second tier of our model.

The Core Areas of Performance Competence

These three **Core Areas of Performance** of the second tier of our model include:

1. Product & Service Line Design
2. Product & Service Line Development
3. Product & Service Line Deployment

Let's take a quick, closer look at each. These are the heart of a Curriculum Manager's job – as they are the heart and **reason for being** of any L&D organization in an Enterprise.

C1- Product & Service Line Design is about the design or architecture of the entire set of content offerings, both current and future, addressing the existing content and the gap content – all based on the Performance Competence Requirements of your priority Target Audiences, audiences that I label as PUSH or PULL.

> This is what I refer to as **Curriculum Architecture Design** – something I have been doing as an external consultant since 1982. And using a methodology that was first published in September of 1984 – in Training Magazine.

C2- Product & Service Line Development is about the development or acquisition – the make or buy – of the products and services to be offered.

> This is typically referred to as ADDIE: Analysis, Design, Development, Implementation and Evaluation of Instructional Content, but is known by other names as well, including SAT: Structured Approach to Training.
>
> ADDIE and SAT are just the instructional design world's version of New Product Development – and if you are familiar with that or any engineering world's approach to their work you will see the parallels.

C3- Product & Service Line Deployment is about the deployment of content for PUSH – and making content available for access for both PUSH and PULL Target Audiences – covering all of the products and services that are offered and are to be offered at some point. Content is also either pushed or pulled, or both. It may be deployed synchronously and accessible asynchronously. It might be of any media or mode.

What is appropriate in terms of media and mode is always Context Specific for each Target Audience – meaning that it may be unique from one audience to the next – meaning that your approach might require you to be flexible and offer certain content in more than one manner, more than one media and mode.

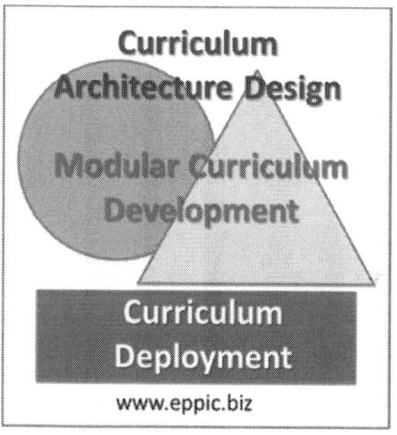

At the Core of a Curriculum Manager's
Performance Competence Requirements
are the architecture, development and deployment of
performance-enabling
Instructional and Informational Content

PUSH and PULL

PUSH Target Audiences refers to the most critical jobs in the most critical processes of your Enterprise – or for that portion for which you have responsibility for as a Curriculum Manager. It is the PUSH Target Audiences that should be invested in in terms of L&D content.

PULL Target Audiences refers to everybody else. Their needs for L&D should not be addressed directly. But they should be able, at their managements' discretion, to access content deliberately developed/ acquired for PUSH audiences.

In a resource constrained world, with a business-like focus on ROI, L&D should be done for the sake of the shareholder, and not for the sake of learning.

If there isn't a significant ROI for an L&D effort, it should be forgone so that the Enterprise can make wiser investments elsewhere.

It is NOT about Learning – it IS about Business. It is about the Performance Competence where there are Risks to be avoided and Rewards to be achieved. It is that simple.

Content Context Check

- Does the role of Curriculum Manager in your Enterprise include these Core responsibilities?

- If they do not, should they?

- Are they currently the responsibility of some other job – and if so, is that working well enough?

Core AoPs Overview Summary

These three **Core Areas of Performance** include management activities that are the heart of the job and the department/ function/ organization itself.

Here leaders and mangers are focused on planning and working for the short term needs of their Target Audiences – and managing for their "in the moment" needs, and includes:

> **Planning the Work** – which is about deciding what gets done and by whom and when.
>
> **Assigning the Work** – which addresses the communications of the work assignment to those being assigned, and perhaps to everyone else as well.
>
> **Monitoring the Work** – which focuses on the follow up monitoring of work processes and/or work products to insure that everything is okay. If not, see the next activity.
>
> **Troubleshooting the Work** – which addresses the following up on any work products or processes' discrepancies to resolve them.

These are part of any manager's job: the planning, assigning, monitoring, and troubleshooting of the work of their subordinates and their subordinate organizations.

The next part of the job involves putting everything else in place – the **Support** processes, the people, and the environmental supports – so that the **Leadership** and **Core** goals, plans and budgets achieve the desired end goals via the design, development and deployment of enabling L&D

content. And that is to deliberately enable the Performance Competence of the PUSH Target Audiences.

These three Core AoPs of a Curriculum Manager will be covered in greater detail in chapters 8 – 10.

You will do your adaptation thinking, as needed, when reading those chapters.

Next we move to the 3rd tier of our model.

The Support Areas of Performance Competence

These four **Support** Areas of Performance include:

1- Process Design & Redesign
2- Human Assets
3- Environmental Assets
4- Special Assignments

The **Support** Areas of Performance are about putting "everything in place" so that the leadership goals and plan and budgets achieve the desired end goals; so that there is something to plan, assign, monitor, and troubleshoot.

Let's now look a little deeper at each of the AoPs in tier 3 of the model.

S1- Process Design & Redesign is about making changes to the existing processes in terms of their outputs, steps, inputs, individual contributors' roles/responsibilities, etc., or in designing new processes.

> Approaches from the Quality world that may be adapted to aid in your Process Design efforts include Quality Function Deployment to define the products/

outputs of the process, Lean to streamline the process, and Six Sigma to reduce variation in the process as a means to reduce variation in the products/ outputs, among other methods, tools and techniques.

S2- Human Assets Management is about the acquisition, development, appraisal and compensation/rewarding of the human assets, the human resources, the Performers who are at times formal Learners.

> These are about using the typically HR systems that support you in supporting the Enterprise's training and development and performance support needs.

S3- Environmental Assets Management is about the acquisition, development, and maintenance of all of the non-human assets necessary to the support humans in performing in the processes.

> Putting all of the necessary environmental supports for your people is a critical part of a Curriculum Manager's job.

S4- Special Assignments is about the "other duties as assigned" responsibilities of management.

> This is admittedly a catch-all Area of Performance. But if your role as a Curriculum Manager includes them, it may be helpful to address here in case it is a distraction and should be shed. Or if it is truly important, then it too should be enabled in some manner.

Content Context Check

- Does the role of Curriculum Manager in your Enterprise include these Support responsibilities?

- If they do not, should they?
- Are they currently the responsibility of some other job – and if so, is that working well enough?

Support AoPs Overview Summary

Leaders and managers are responsible for putting processes in place and the people assets in place and the non-people assets in place to get the priority job done for the Customers and Stakeholders with the resources provided.

The Planning & Management of these AoPs for a Curriculum Manager also includes the following:

> **Planning the Work** – which is about deciding what gets done and by whom and when.
>
> **Assigning the Work** – which addresses the communications of the work assignment.
>
> **Monitoring the Work** – which focuses on the follow up monitoring of work processes and/or work products to insure that everything is okay.
>
> **Troubleshooting the Work** addresses the following up on work product or process discrepancies to resolve them.

These four **Support** AoPs of a Curriculum Manager will be covered in greater detail in chapters 11 – 14.

You will do your thinking about your specific adaptation requirements, as needed by your context, when reading those chapters.

And you will be prompted to think further about all of the adaptations that you might require at the end of the book as well.

Chapter Summary & Transition

This chapter was intended to quickly overview the model being used in this book to frame all of the possible roles and responsibilities of an Enterprise Curriculum Manager – a role who is concerned with the performance sustainment and the improvement of PUSH Target Audiences, chosen by the Customers and Stakeholders, via performance-based L&D of any blend.

Although your job title may be different than "Curriculum Manager" – it is the roles and responsibilities we are addressing here.

And those roles and responsibilities will most likely need your adaptations - just as you may need to adapt this content to a different job title than this book uses for this role.

Again, the model that we are using is presented next.

Curriculum Manager's Areas of Performance Competence Model

LEADERSHIP AoPs - Planning & Management
- Stakeholder Needs Assessment & Alignment
- Strategic Planning
- Operations Planning
- Results Measurement
- Improvement Planning
- Communications

CORE AoPs - Planning & Management
- Product & Service Line Design
- Product & Service Line Development
- Product & Service Line Deployment

SUPPORT AoPs - Planning & Management
- Process Design and Redesign
- Human Assets
- Environmental Assets
- Special Assignments

Adapted from the Management Areas of Performance Model
©2002 Guy W. Wallace

This chapter logically leads to the next, but your needs may cause you to want to skip around.

The list of chapters and their pages numbers are presented next for your personal navigation needs and desires.

1   What Does a Curriculum Manager Do?   1

2	AoP: Stakeholder Needs Assessment & Alignment	27
3	AoP: Strategic Planning & Management	53
4	AoP: Operations Planning & Management	65
5	AoP: Results Measurement	79
6	AoP: Improvement Planning	95
7	AoP: Communications	107
8	AoP: Product & Service Line Design	120
9	AoP: Product & Service Line Development	143
10	AoP: Product & Service Line Deployment	169
11	AoP: Process Design & Redesign	193
12	AoP: Human Assets	203
13	AoP: Environmental Assets	222
14	AoP: Special Assignments	241
15	Summary & Close	247
16	Additional Related Resources & References	254

You may or may not need to read or review all chapters, depending on how your Enterprise has defined the role that is most closely related to what I have termed here as the **Curriculum Manager**.

Proceed accordingly!

Suggested Chapter Reflection & Reaction

I would suggest that prior to jumping into whichever chapter meets your needs that you give pause for a short moment to reflect on the following and perhaps make some notes:

- What are your own "ah-ha's" so far?

- How would you need to think about this model differently than it is presented?

- What language changes and deletions or additions might you need to make?

- What are some of the implications for you that you see already?

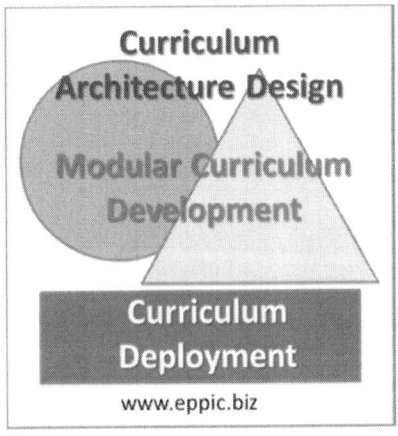

At the Core of a Curriculum Manager's
Performance Competence Requirements
are the architecture, development and deployment of
performance-enabling
Instructional and Informational Content

2 – AREA OF PERFORMANCE: STAKEHOLDER NEEDS ASSESSMENT & ALIGNMENT

Chapter Overview

Read or scan this chapter if your role as a Curriculum Manager is concerned with:

Stakeholder Needs Assessment & Alignment – which involves gathering various Stakeholder inputs regarding their needs, and gathering feedback on how well you are doing in meeting those needs, given the resources provided and all of the other priorities you face.

L1- Stakeholder Needs Assessment & Alignment is where you insure your relevancy to the Enterprise.

This chapter will overview this Area of Performance and then explore in detail a **Governance & Advisory System** and its set of **Processes** for accomplishing this very important aspect of a Curriculum Manager's responsibilities.

This is a responsibility that is itself a measure of good stewardship practices and leads to aligned efforts and significant ROI. A responsibility that if not addressed – leads to misalignment – and poor Returns on Investments – which will lead to Stakeholder frustrations – **and that can't be good for any Curriculum Manager**.

As you read through this chapter keep in mind your context will most likely require you to adapt this content – or to adapt your context to this content.

This chapter fits within the overall flow of the model as presented in the following graphic.

> # Curriculum Manager's Areas of Performance Competence Model
>
> **LEADERSHIP AoPs - Planning & Management**
> - ❏ Stakeholder Needs Assessment & Alignment
> - ❏ Strategic Planning
> - ❏ Operations Planning
> - ❏ Results Measurement
> - ❏ Improvement Planning
> - ❏ Communications
>
> **CORE AoPs - Planning & Management**
> - ❏ Product & Service Line Design
> - ❏ Product & Service Line Development
> - ❏ Product & Service Line Deployment
>
> **SUPPORT AoPs - Planning & Management**
> - ❏ Process Design and Redesign
> - ❏ Human Assets
> - ❏ Environmental Assets
> - ❏ Special Assignments
>
> Adapted from the Management Areas of Performance Model
> ©2002 Guy W. Wallace

AoP: L1- Stakeholder Needs Assessment & Alignment

AoP Overview

The **L1- Stakeholder Needs Assessment & Alignment** Area of Performance involves leaders and managers in gathering "Voice of the various Stakeholders" and then determining, collaboratively or not, what to do about the messages in the voices.

The Stakeholder voices will provide

- **Requests** for products/services and specific requirements for that Stakeholder

- **Feedback** on how well you are doing (or not) in meeting those requests

- **Insights** into their future needs

The Stakeholders

Your Stakeholders may have the following typical needs/issues for you to deal align with and serve:

Government Stakeholders
- This Stakeholder provides laws and regulations that must be complied with under the threat of financial penalty or jail time for non-compliance.

How are you supporting those needs?

Are helping to protect as well as improve the Enterprise?

Owner/Shareholder Stakeholders
- This Stakeholder has expectations of a financial nature and/or social issues/demands.

How are you insuring significant Returns on the

Investments being made in Content? Are you a good steward of shareholder equity?

Executive/Management Stakeholders
- This Stakeholder has a fiduciary responsibility to the owners/shareholders, and compliance responsibilities to the governments, service responsibilities to the customers, leadership responsibilities to the employees, fairness responsibilities to the suppliers, and various social responsibilities to the communities in which the business operates.

How are you helping with all of these? Do your Enterprise executives know what you are doing here – and what you are not doing here, and why not?

Customer Stakeholders
- This Stakeholder requires real value for the products/services that your Enterprise renders to them.

How are you supporting their needs? And should you be supporting the external Customers' needs for L&D, or not?

Employee Stakeholders
- This Stakeholder has a need for development of their Performance Competence, for a safe workplace, for fair wages for their performance, and for equal opportunity under the law.

How are you supporting these internal customers, the PUSH Learners and the management? Are you designing and making available the content for PUSH Target Audiences to the PULL Target Audiences as well? Should you?

Industry Group Stakeholders
- This Stakeholder has an interest in compliance with Industry norms and standards, as agreed to by the suppliers, customers and perhaps government/regulators in their marketplaces.

How are you supporting their requirements? And, should you be supporting their needs – or the needs of those internal Enterprise groups who interface with these external groups?

Supplier Stakeholders
- This Stakeholder has a need for fairness in terms of their business opportunities with your Enterprise, and for timely payments for services and products delivered.

How are you supporting those? And, should you be supporting their needs – or the needs of those internally who interface with these groups?

Community Stakeholders
- This Stakeholder has various economic and social issues, at the local, national or globally levels – issues that may or may not have found their way into law/regulations/codes – yet.

How are you supporting their needs? And, should you be supporting their needs – or the needs of those internally who interface with these groups?

There are many Stakeholder Categories and constituencies

within each Category. Your focus as a Curriculum Manager may be wide or narrow – by charge or charter.

You might have only one primary Target Audience and therefore a narrower set of Stakeholders, or you might have many Target Audiences and therefore many Stakeholders.

It is up to you to proactively understand who your Stakeholders are and what their needs and desires are and then work with them to best meet their needs given likely resources constraints – and potential conflicts in their requirements.

Unless, of course, someone has laid all of this out to you and it is already crystal clear to you and everybody else.

Typical AoP Outputs

The Curriculum Manager "**outputs**" of this Area of Performance typically include:

- **Assessments of all Needs** - and a balancing of any conflicts in the needs.
- **Governance** – decisions and directives on what market segments to serve and not serve, based on the balancing of the many Stakeholder voices – and then providing clear, specific directives to your team and to all other Enterprise functions, systems/processes and people throughout your "sphere of responsibility/ accountability."

Examples include directives/ marching orders for the rest of the L&D function that are long-term, medium-term, and/or short-term, such as:

- Let's not go into that customer segment now (or ever)

- Let's extend the life of that training product
- Let's buy that L&D product and customize it rather than develop it from scratch
- Create a new role/ job in our team
- Promote this person in our organization
- Hire that supplier resource
- Fire this other resource
- Find a new set of suppliers and broaden (or narrow) our overall supplier base
- Change/improve this process but not that one

Typical AoP Tasks

The Curriculum Manager "**tasks**" related to this Area of Performance and to the outputs above, typically include:

- Meeting with appropriate Stakeholders - depending on your and others' levels and responsibilities/ accountabilities - or others in your Enterprise with the responsibility to exchange data and information to and from certain groups.

    It wouldn't do to have every Enterprise manager interacting with each of the regulatory agencies of the governments in the countries where you operate.

- Making business decisions about the appropriateness or not of the L&D products and the systems and processes you have in place, in conjunction with and collaboratively with some or all of your Stakeholder groups.

- Communicating clear, specific messages to the appropriate group(s) through the appropriate channel(s).

AoP Systems & Processes Overview

Next we will look at a formal System for addressing this AoP of **Stakeholder Needs Assessment and Alignment**:

- **Governance & Advisory System**

There are both formal and informal means for connecting with your Customers and other Stakeholders as a Curriculum Manager to help you better assess and understand their needs and get yourself appropriately aligned.

Discussing a more formal means to this and then discussing the informal means to accomplish this is easier than the alternative; so we will start there – with a formal approach first, and then discuss how to do this less formally second.

This approach involves two processes of what I call a Governance and Advisory System. You may call them anything appropriate for your context.

This system is the central, driving force behind the strategies and success of a business-based approach to L&D. Without something akin to this in place, it's unlikely that the other systems/ processes leveraged by a Curriculum Manager will truly have real return on the investments made and return economic value add. **This is where and how YOU get aligned.**

In this model an Advisory Process provides a forum for your L&D Customer groups to make informed business decisions about their needs and then they communicate that to those governing decision-makers – which will decide on which L&D products to build and which maintenance needs to address – and which needs and wants to forego. These are business decisions – and not everything needed will get attended to.

The Governance Processes give the organization's executive-level leadership specific process mechanisms to affect L&D strategies, tactics, and to direct all resource allocations in order to achieve the worthy business results of their choosing.

L&D systems must be driven and governed by the voice of their Customers and the other key Stakeholders, as they, your Customers and other key Stakeholders, formalize their plans and manage their activities.

This system's processes organize and formalize this up and down communication with those key Enterprise Stakeholders – Customers being just one of those types of Stakeholders, as covered earlier in this chapter.

This model channels *advice* up from the L&D internal and external (if appropriate) marketplace customers to the Enterprise leadership for their consideration and final decisions for resource allocations.

Then those decisions and resource allocations are channeled *down* from the leaders of the Enterprise in response to that advice – advice otherwise known as requests for resources.

The following Processes of this System will be reviewed next:

- Governance Processes
- Advisory Processes

Let's start at the top.

The Governance Processes

Processes Purpose - the Governance Processes organize the executives of the Enterprise for the purpose of directing both the overall L&D system and the specific efforts to expend the limited resources allocated, toward only the high-priority/high-payback needs.

Processes Description - These processes organize the Enterprise's executives into a board of governors for the L&D system and charges them with stewardship for the overall L&D investment. They will act on behalf of the Enterprise leadership, all other Stakeholders, and especially the shareholders—the owners.

The board of governors, with advice, will rule L&D.

Business decisions will rule.

No more undo attention will be paid to the "low-hanging fruit" with its mass appeal.

If these executives target L&D for only significant return on investment, or economic value add, as measured by human performance and business process performance metrics, "time management" probably won't be given the time of day.

Generic programs, such as most of the Time Management programs I have seen in over 30 years, treat everyone as if they have the same performance context. And they do not. So the content offered, while having "face validity" does not have "performance context validity" and therefore is unlikely to have a positive effect on the Learners – when they go back to the job and perform.

Research shows that only about 15% of the population can learn out of context and apply what they learned in another context (from a phone call conversation with Richard E. Clark, PhD in 2007).

If the L&D effort and investment aren't projected to provide a significant financial return now or later, they simply are not attended to. The body count of personnel to be affected by the L&D isn't the driver for prioritization and expenditures.

Just because L&D professionals—who were recruited and selected for their skill in systematically uncovering knowledge and skill needs—uncover those needs, does not mean that the Enterprise should meet those needs. Only those needs with potential returns above the corporate "hurdle rate" for return on investment, or that make other business sense, should be addressed.

The process performance-biased/oriented organization does not strive for L&D that will maximize the "butts in seats" or "butts on sites" measures (the key measures for the lowest of the "low-hanging fruit"). Nor does it automatically address the current, popular, faddish spin on "age-old wisdom" packaged in up-to-date, sexy, newfangled technology, just because that's currently in vogue.

If it won't result in better process performance, it isn't done.

The only way to ensure that the L&D system is addressing the critical and highly important L&D needs – business needs – is to systematically engage the leaders of the Enterprise and to double-check with them regarding the findings of our systematic analyses.

They then will cherry-pick what to address and will also be involved in the discussion of the alternative approaches with which to affect the high-payback situations.

After all, they live with the consequences – the results of those decisions.

Depending on the overall complexity of the Enterprise, the Governance System may be a hierarchy of committees/councils of the key leaders of the Enterprise, or it could be one single group. It depends on the similarity or differences in the "business units" and their people's L&D needs. Most companies can do with one single board of governors.

In addition to their day jobs, the "governors" are charged with the collateral duty of overseeing the entire L&D system.

They can meet in an established forum, where L&D topics are added to their existing agenda, or their responsibilities can be carried out through a new committee/council structure established exclusively to manage the L&D system and its limited resources.

The top committee/council might typically meet twice a year after getting this system and process up and running.

The L&D board of governors' objective is to enable the human assets of the Enterprise to better perform in all priority, critical business processes. It is consistent with the goals and objectives of the Enterprise's board of directors, which are typically to maximize shareholder return over the long run.

They allocate the Enterprise's resources – headcount, facilities, equipment, and dollars – as a means to an end. The end target is high performance in targeted business operations or in all operations.

It's a business decision.

This team of executives establishes sub-processes to:

- Communicate the current challenges and opportunities of the business.
- Communicate the general business plan.
- Communicate the L&D goals in measurable terms linked to the business plan.
- Establish and oversee the Advisory Processes.
- Provide resources and oversee L&D programs and projects to build the required infrastructure.
- Provide resources and oversee L&D programs and projects to build and maintain the high-payback L&D products and services.
- Collect measurement data and direct improvement efforts at targeted areas.
- Champion the targeted development of relevant, economic value adding, Enterprise competence.

The L&D **Governance** Processes work closely with the L&D **Advisory** Processes.

Where the Advisory Processes provide advice to the Enterprise leadership board of governors from their parochial needs and perspectives, the Governance Processes then makes the business decisions, which might be simply to agree and then fund the requests from the L&D Advisory Processes.

More on the L&D Advisory Processes is provided later in this chapter.

The board of governors is more than just the final decision body regarding the allocation of *most-likely* limited Enterprise resources.

They are the ultimate stewards of shareholder equity who target the results, redirect efforts as needed, and hold the entire system accountable, just as they are ultimately accountable to the Enterprise shareholders. I like to think of them as follows when they do their due diligence:

Ladies and gentlemen of the L&D Board of Governors, please place your strategic bets.

The L&D Governance Processes interfaces with many of the other systems and processes portrayed in the Curriculum Manager's Areas of Performance model, in order to provide this critical direction and obtain the inputs and feedback necessary to get and stay aligned. This is where the L&D function's "marching orders" come from.

Are Your Governance Processes Broken? Clues and Cues

Your Governance Processes may be broken if:

- The priorities and projects of the often change midstream, with little business rhyme or reason.
- There is little energy or enthusiasm for many of your projects, and it is difficult to get the internal customer engaged and involved in timely and meaningful ways.
- Projects are under-resourced or improperly resourced (any "body" "will do").
- Projects have unrealistic cycle times.
- Projects themselves have no structure and do not seem to be scheduled activities on the calendars of the customer to be served.
- L&D is not a major component of either the overall business plan, or the HR plan, or the business plans for the other business units and functions.

Governance Processes Summary

The L&D Governance Processes govern.

The leaders get together to go through the processes, with guidance and support from L&D professionals – especially the Curriculum Managers, to make business decisions regarding L&D.

The board of governors of the L&D system directs the overall L&D system to meet the needs of the Enterprise, wherever the cost of nonconformance or return on investment situation dictates.

But where will these leaders get the insight into what issues, problems, and opportunities exist that have high-payback potential? Where will they get such advice?

From the L&D Advisory Processes, which we'll cover next.

The Advisory Processes

Advisory Processes Purpose

The L&D Advisory Processes are a set of advisory committees/councils that identify and communicate to the L&D Board of Governors (BoG) their parochial, high-payback, potential targets for L&D that need resourcing.

Then decisions are made by that BoG as to who gets what.

The Advisory Councils then oversee and conduct the approved, targeted L&D project efforts for their area of concern.

The advisory committees/councils are immediately below the decision-making body of the board of governors of the L&D Governance Processes.

Advisory Processes Description

The advisory groups represent the needs of the business or the functional groups that they represent.

These processes are intended to look out for the parochial needs of the individual business units, and/or functions, and/or major processes of the Enterprise, and the "expertise disciplines" as well – but that representation, for a complex organization, might take on a functional versus organizational orientation.

Their specific structure and focus depends on how these customer groups are structured. That could be along:

- Business unit lines
- Functional lines
- Process lines
- Discipline lines

As always, it depends on the organization being served.

Form should follow function. But what function?

My preference for structure would typically go toward functional/discipline – over a process-based set of councils – due to the similarity of L&D content needed within a functional or discipline group – it's just leads to more **sharable content**. And that reduces first and life cycle costs.

Ignoring the value of a functional orientation was a mistake of the quality movement in my opinion. Taking away the "homeroom" of peers in their function and strewing them up and down the processes as organizations were suggested to do in a reorganization into the natural process flows – was an anti-social move from the perspective of many of these citizens of the Enterprise.

Can you not be functionally-organized and process-centric in your thinking and perspective?

I tend to favor Advisory groups organized, for example, in Marketing, Engineering, Sales, Manufacturing, Distribution, Finance, HR, etc.

Plus one on Management & Leadership.

I would be both discipline-centric and process-centric.

Enterprise L&D needs may more often fall in line with a *functional/discipline* segmentation scheme that recognizes and addresses the uniqueness of the focus of varied business units.

The opportunity to see common needs, as well as unique needs (for, say, marketing professionals or welders), is easiest when the L&D Advisory Processes and their Councils are process-oriented, but functionally-organized.

The performance orientation of any and all L&D content should ensure that the specific process-related needs for those disciplines will be properly addressed.

No matter how you structure the Advisory Processes, the goal is to elicit the "performance-based" needs from the appropriate targets within the Enterprise in a systematic manner so that business decisions can be made about real, high-payback needs. And then to meet those needs.

With priorities in hand from the Curriculum Architecture Design-like processes, the Advisory Processes drives the approved efforts forward, according to the level of resources that the Enterprise is willing and able to invest in those targets, based on the anticipated/projected returns on those investments.

It is still a business decision, even for a learning organization.

The Advisory System directs the product and service "lines" definition and macro-design processes, in terms of which priority PUSH Target Audiences need to be addressed with L&D products and services. This is accomplished for those Advisory Councils via the establishment of Project Steering Teams (PST) for their key efforts.

The team members for these PSTs are handpicked by the advisory committees for the Curriculum Architecture Design-like efforts.

Project Steering Teams may be disbanded after those projects have been completed, or they may be kept intact for the follow-on efforts, when the high-priority gaps of a the Curriculum Architecture Design are addressed post-CAD by the L&D Product and Service Line Development/Acquisition processes – covered later. They would then oversee those project efforts as well – great for continuity.

The designated Project Steering Teams populate the high-priority projects, established by their Advisory Councils, with members for the various teams on those projects, such as Analysis Teams, Design Teams, etc. They then oversee each of those projects to ensure high-payback returns on the investments leading to: economic value add.

The Communications System – covered later - communicates their messages consistent about these project efforts.

The L&D Advisory Processes interfaces with many of the other L&D systems and processes used to accomplish the Curriculum Manager's Areas of Performance. It can be very complex.

Are Your Advisory Processes Broken? Clues and Cues

Your Advisory Processes may be broken if:

- The advice given to the ultimate, executive decision-makers regarding resource allocations is happening without the Curriculum Manager's active, structured involvement, and is more political than rational/process-performance based.
- There is no macro-development plan for addressing key Target Audiences.
- Most projects are "one-offs," one-shot efforts, which do not lead to anything cohesive for key Target Audiences.
- Development projects are conducted without a clear understanding of their target's cost of conformance and cost of nonconformance, for forecasting the life-cycle costs that will be incurred over time to offer this product/service to the internal marketplace.
- You feel that you have to continually roll with the punches and are constantly going from one project "fire" to another.

Advisory Processes Summary

The Advisory Processes are where the business drivers come from for key content development and acquisition efforts.

A Curriculum Manager puts themself into the hands of its Customers and Stakeholders for the key decisions regarding targets and value; and the Customers and other Stakeholders control the overall processes on how targets are determined, and conduct the value determinations for estimating ROI.

The Advisory Processes ensure that the voice of the Customers and other Stakeholders are heard in decision-making. It's a voice too often heard way off in the distance and just "plain too late" to have an impact.

It's voices crying out – not in uniform harmony – but in discord. It sounds like "noise" unless you know how to break it down and interpret them.

This set of processes is one of the most critical to any Curriculum Manager.

It pays homage to the adage of "know thy customer" and "listen, listen, and then listen some more."

The Advisory Processes provides everyone with just the right forum with the right people for that to occur.

An Informal Approach to Governance & Advisory Systems

The formal approaches we just covered could be approached less formally.

Enterprise leaders and Stakeholders and your direct Customers can be interviewed in their offices or at lunch/dinners, and the business issues and needs solicited and feedback gathered on prior effort.

This trick is getting everyone to consensus via a series of meetings where the Curriculum Manager is the go-between. It can be done in non-complex situations.

AoP Summary

This Area of Performance is about assessing and aligning with both your internal Customers and your other internal Stakeholders.

The formal System's Processes for addressing the Curriculum Manager's responsibilities for your **Stakeholder Needs Assessment & Alignment** Area of Performance include:

- Governance Processes
- Advisory Processes

Part of your responsibility as a Curriculum Manager is to adopt and/ or adapt what has been presented here for your own context. Hopefully this has provided you with some guidance for doing that.

How Are You Currently Performing This Area of Performance Competence?

Regarding the Stakeholder Needs Assessment and Alignment AoP…

How are you currently **Planning this Work** – how are you deciding what needs to get done, and by whom, and when?

What, if anything, needs to change?

How are you currently **Assigning this Work** – and how are you communicating the expectations of the work assignment?

What, if anything, needs to change?

How are you currently **Monitoring this Work** – and how are you focusing on the follow-up monitoring of work process and/or work product to insure that everything is okay?

What, if anything, needs to change?

How are you currently **Troubleshooting this Work** – how are you following up for the work products or work process where you have spotted discrepancies, in order to resolve them?

What, if anything, needs to change?

Chapter Summary & Transition

This chapter was intended to address **Stakeholder Needs Assessment & Alignment** – where you determine all Stakeholder requirements, both the short-term and long-term, and then balance any and all conflicts.

This is *the most important* Area of Performance for a Curriculum Manager.

You could be great at content design and development and deployment – but if you are not aligned with the key Stakeholders – none of that matters.

This chapter logically leads to the next, but your needs may cause you to want to skip around.

The list of chapters and their pages numbers are presented next for your personal navigation needs and desires.

1	What Does a Curriculum Manager Do?	1
2	AoP: Stakeholder Needs Assessment & Alignment	27
3	AoP: Strategic Planning & Management	53
4	AoP: Operations Planning & Management	65
5	AoP: Results Measurement	79
6	AoP: Improvement Planning	95
7	AoP: Communications	107
8	AoP: Product & Service Line Design	120
9	AoP: Product & Service Line Development	143
10	AoP: Product & Service Line Deployment	169
11	AoP: Process Design & Redesign	193
12	AoP: Human Assets	203
13	AoP: Environmental Assets	222
14	AoP: Special Assignments	241

| 15 | Summary & Close | 247 |
| 16 | Additional Related Resources & References | 254 |

Suggested Chapter Reflection & Reaction

I would suggest that prior to jumping into whichever chapter meets your needs that you give pause for a moment to reflect on the following and make some notes:

- What are your own "ah-ha's" so far?

- Are there processes in place that appropriately align you to the needs of your Stakeholders? If not, what is the cost of the problem or opportunity, and what are the potential Returns for any Investments for improving these?

- Are your processes formal enough, too formal, or just right?

- How would you need to think about this model differently than it is presented?

- What language changes and deletions or additions might you need to make?

- What are all of the implications for you and your L&D function thus far?

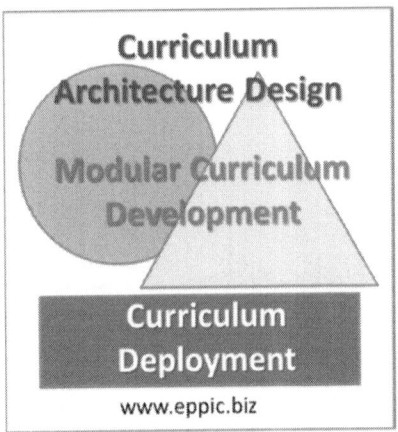

At the Core of a Curriculum Manager's
Performance Competence Requirements
are the architecture, development and deployment of
performance-enabling
Instructional and Informational Content

3 - AREA OF PERFORMANCE: STRATEGIC PLANNING

Chapter Overview

Read or scan this chapter if you are concerned with:

- **Strategic Planning** - setting strategic goals and developing plans to achieve those goals, in alignment with your Customers and other Stakeholders

This chapter is intended to provide you with some details related to this Area of Performance (AoP) including a formal System and Processes for accomplishing this work – which you may adopt, or may need to adapt.

1.2- Strategic Planning – which is where the long-term goals are established to meet the long-term needs of the balanced Stakeholders' requirements.

As you read through this chapter keep in mind your potential need to adapt this content to your context – or to adapt your context to this content.

This chapter fits within the overall flow of the model as presented in the following graphic.

Curriculum Manager's Areas of Performance Competence Model

LEADERSHIP AoPs - Planning & Management
- ❏ Stakeholder Needs Assessment & Alignment
- ❏ Strategic Planning
- ❏ Operations Planning
- ❏ Results Measurement
- ❏ Improvement Planning
- ❏ Communications

CORE AoPs - Planning & Management
- ❏ Product & Service Line Design
- ❏ Product & Service Line Development
- ❏ Product & Service Line Deployment

SUPPORT AoPs - Planning & Management
- ❏ Process Design and Redesign
- ❏ Human Assets
- ❏ Environmental Assets
- ❏ Special Assignments

Adapted from the Management Areas of Performance Model
©2002 Guy W. Wallace

AoP: L2- Strategic Planning

AoP Overview

The **Strategic Planning** Area of Performance involves development of a Strategic Plan based on the voices of your Stakeholders and all of their strategic plans.

Typical AoP Outputs

The Curriculum Manager's "**outputs**" for this Area of Performance include:

- **Strategic Plan Inputs**: summaries of all drivers for your strategic plan

- **Your Strategic Plan**: a multi-year plan reflecting a balance of all of the drivers

Typical AoP Tasks

The "**tasks**" of this Area of Performance, related to the outputs above, typically include:

- Meeting with your appropriate Stakeholders to gather their strategic plans' implications as inputs for your strategic plan. These Stakeholders include your key staff members too!

- Developing your plan

- Communicating/reviewing your plan, selling as needed, and updating as necessary

AoP Systems & Processes Overview

Next we will look at a formal System for addressing this AoP:

- **Strategic Planning Systems**

A Curriculum Manager's strategic plans are driven by the strategic and tactical plans of their key Customers and other Stakeholders.

From a performance standpoint, the system should guide, enable, and support the Customer's businesses in achieving their targeted goals with high-impact L&D content where appropriate.

A Curriculum Manager and their staff must help their customers figure this out if there isn't another process in place governing everyone's Strategic Planning processes and outputs. They must provide a viable process for achieving the determination of these "mission-critical" strategic needs. It is in their best interest to do so.

This system is effective only if it helps direct your Training, Learning & Knowledge Management system to prepare to address both today's and tomorrow's business needs – the showstoppers and make-or-break opportunities of the Enterprise.

This system uncovers exactly where key Stakeholders and Customers want their strategic bets placed.

It also rationally determines the resource requirements for addressing those strategic needs and then addresses your organization's current capability and capacity – or lack thereof – to carry out those plans to meet the Customers' and Stakeholders' needs, both now and in the future.

This system's processes organize all of the strategic planning for Training, Learning & Knowledge Management to ensure that their plans and efforts are consistent and in alignment with the strategic plans of the critical elements of the Enterprise.

This system is tied to the Enterprise's strategic planning system if one exists. It seeks an "early warning" for the L&D team for all requests that might come their way in the short-term and long-term.

The following Processes of that System will be reviewed next:

- The Strategic Plans Surveillance Processes
- The Strategic Planning Processes

Let's look at the first of these.

Strategic Planning Surveillance Processes

Surveillance Processes Purpose

The Strategic Plans Surveillance Processes ensures that the Training, Learning & Knowledge Management system, including the leadership and their Governance and Advisory System, is acutely aware of all of the strategic business drivers of the various components of the Enterprise and takes those into account when generating their own strategic and operational plans and activities.

Surveillance Processes Description

The Strategic Plans Surveillance Processes deliberately and systematically engages the key elements of the Enterprise, typically via the Governance and Advisory structures, to determine those *show-stopping* needs that will help or hinder the accomplishment of the strategic intent for those business-critical needs. Not all needs across the Enterprise are equal in their potential payback.

This proactive uncovering of the potential Enterprise investment requirements for content, as led by Enterprise leadership in collaboration with both the Advisory and Governance Processes elements, is critical to the viability of the Curriculum content. The system and processes put in place should formally elicit the annual strategic plans of the Enterprise.

This will lead to uncovering exactly where the key Stakeholders, including the shareholders of the Enterprise, would want their strategic bets placed.

The Strategic Plans Surveillance Processes interface with many of the other Training, Learning & Knowledge Management systems' processes.

Are Your Strategic Plans Surveillance Processes Broken? Clues and Cues

Your Strategic Plans Surveillance Processes may be broken if:

- You have no clue about the high-payback strategies of the key Customer segments of your Enterprise.
- Your resources that help you meet the strategic needs of your Customers and other key Stakeholders are not seen as strategic themselves.

Processes Summary

The Strategic Plans Surveillance Processes ensures a clear, visible understanding of the strategic issues and their related needs by the Curriculum Manager and/or their staff and also the Governance and Advisory System members. This process deliberately provides knowledge and insight.

The next process describes what to do with that knowledge and insight.

Strategic Planning Processes

Strategic Planning Processes Purpose

The Strategic Planning Processes ensures that the L&D system's own strategic plans are in alignment with, and are supportive of, the key needs of the Enterprise.

Strategic Planning Processes Description

L&D must create its own strategies after assessing its customers' strategic and operational plans and then assessing its current capabilities for carrying them out.

If the L&D system finds itself in a shortfall regarding these capabilities, then it must strategically plan to address the shortfall. It either ignores certain projects or it gets the additional resources needed via the Governance and Advisory System.

After all, it is the Customers and Stakeholders who live with the consequences of not doing efforts that are their priorities – just not high enough in the rankings to get attended to if there isn't enough money and time to deal with them all.

Involving them in these efforts just might help you find additional resources necessary for their needs.

The L&D strategies may need to be updated quarterly, or more often, as the business conditions require. Each Enterprise must dance to the tune of its own unique industry and marketplace situation.

The Strategic Planning Processes should address:

- Strategic plans and needs of L&D's key customers
- Identification of any gaps or excesses of available resources, given current levels and other work plans
- Key gap closing/growth issues of the L&D system
- Strategic plans for projects and other "gap/growth" initiatives necessary to meet those needs

Are Your Strategic Planning Processes Broken? Clues and Cues

Your Strategic Planning Processes may be broken if:

- You have no strategic plan for L&D.
- Your strategies of where you are going and why are not documented.
- Your strategies have not been reviewed and/or approved by the Enterprise leadership as in alignment with the needs of the Enterprise.
- Enterprise executives don't know the strategic value of the organization's contributions from the past, the present, or the future.
- Your team is not aware of and cannot summarize the strategic direction of the L&D organization itself.

Processes Summary

The Strategic Planning Processes ensures that the L&D system is in sync with the main drivers of its customers and has a strategic plan in place to guide its growth and evolution to meet both the current and future needs of the Enterprise.

How important is that to your Enterprise?

AoP Summary

This Area of Performance is about

The formal Systems and Processes for addressing the Curriculum Manager's responsibilities include:

- The Strategic Plans Surveillance Processes
- The Strategic Planning Processes

Part of your responsibility as a Curriculum Manager is to adopt and/ or adapt what has been presented here for your own context.

Hopefully this has provided you with some guidance for doing that.

How Are You Currently Performing This Area of Performance Competence?

Regarding the Strategic Planning Area of Performance…

How are you currently **Planning this Work** – how are you deciding what needs to get done, and by whom, and when?

What, if anything, needs to change?

How are you currently **Assigning this Work** – and the communicating the expectations of the work assignment?

What, if anything, needs to change?

How are you currently **Monitoring this Work** – and focusing on the follow up monitoring of work processes and work products to insure that everything is okay?

What, if anything, needs to change?

How are you currently **Troubleshooting this Work** – and following up for any work products or work processes where you spotted discrepancies, in order to resolve them?

What, if anything, needs to change?

Chapter Summary & Transition

This chapter was intended to address Strategic Planning – where you determine all of your Strategic Planning requirements, based on the Strategic Plans of both your Customers and of your other Stakeholders.

This chapter logically leads to the next, but your needs may cause you to want to skip around.

The list of chapters and their pages numbers are presented next for your personal navigation needs and desires.

1	What Does a Curriculum Manager Do?	1
2	AoP: Stakeholder Needs Assessment & Alignment	27
3	AoP: Strategic Planning & Management	53

4	AoP: Operations Planning & Management	65
5	AoP: Results Measurement	79
6	AoP: Improvement Planning	95
7	AoP: Communications	107
8	AoP: Product & Service Line Design	120
9	AoP: Product & Service Line Development	143
10	AoP: Product & Service Line Deployment	169
11	AoP: Process Design & Redesign	193
12	AoP: Human Assets	203
13	AoP: Environmental Assets	222
14	AoP: Special Assignments	241
15	Summary & Close	247
16	Additional Related Resources & References	254

Suggested Chapter Reflection & Reaction

I would suggest that prior to jumping into whichever chapter meets your needs that you give pause for a moment to reflect on the following and make some notes:

- What are your own "ah-ha's" so far?

- Are your Strategic Planning System and Processes adequate to your needs? If not what is the cost of the problem/ opportunity, or the potential Returns for any Investments for improving these?

- How would you need to think about this model differently than it is presented?

- What language changes and deletions or additions might you need to make?

- What are all of the implications for you and your L&D function thus far?

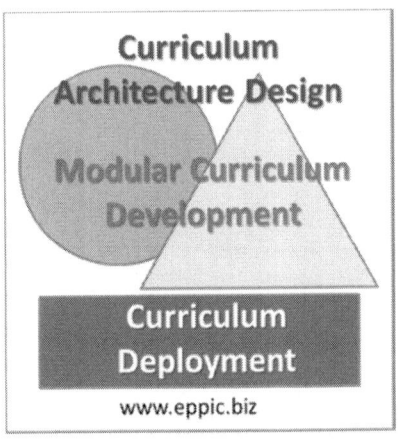

At the Core of a Curriculum Manager's
Performance Competence Requirements
are the architecture, development and deployment of
performance-enabling
Instructional and Informational Content

4 - AREA OF PERFORMANCE: OPERATIONS PLANNING

Chapter Overview

Read or scan this chapter if you are concerned with:

- **Operations Planning** - developing and managing an operations (annual) plan and budget to achieve the assigned year's annual goals/objectives

This chapter is intended to provide you with some details related to this Area of Performance (AoP) including a formal System and Processes for accomplishing this part of a Curriculum Manager's job.

L3- Operations Planning is where the annual planning occurs consistent with the strategic plan and the short-term requirements of the Stakeholders.

This chapter fits within the overall flow of the model as presented in the following graphic.

Curriculum Manager's Areas of Performance Competence Model

LEADERSHIP AoPs - Planning & Management
- ☐ Stakeholder Needs Assessment & Alignment
- ☐ Strategic Planning
- ☐ Operations Planning
- ☐ Results Measurement
- ☐ Improvement Planning
- ☐ Communications

CORE AoPs - Planning & Management
- ☐ Product & Service Line Design
- ☐ Product & Service Line Development
- ☐ Product & Service Line Deployment

SUPPORT AoPs - Planning & Management
- ☐ Process Design and Redesign
- ☐ Human Assets
- ☐ Environmental Assets
- ☐ Special Assignments

Adapted from the Management Areas of Performance Model
©2002 Guy W. Wallace

As you read through this chapter keep in mind your potential need to adapt this content to your context – or to adapt your context to this content.

AoP: L3- Operations Planning

AoP Overview

The **Operations Planning** Area of Performance involves developing a plan and budget for operations covering the year based on given goals/objectives for the year and the existing strategic plan.

It should follow the format provided by your Enterprise.

Typical AoP Outputs

The Curriculum Manager's "**outputs**" of this Area of Performance typically include:

- Annual Operations Plan and Budget, with breakdowns perhaps by quarter and month

Typical AoP Tasks

The "**tasks**" of this Area of Performance, related to the outputs above, typically include:

- Developing an Operations Plan and Budget draft
- Reviewing the plan and budget with your management
- Updating the Operations Plan and Budget per feedback received
- Communicating the final plan with specific messages to the appropriate group(s) through the

appropriate channel(s)
- Following the plan, monitoring other implementation, and adjusting/updating it as necessary

AoP Systems & Processes Overview

Next we will look at a formal System for addressing this AoP:

- **The Operations Planning Systems & Processes**

The L&D organization must be ready to re-aim and re-allocate as the business's strategic drivers change, and it should do so in a planned manner.

This is the system in which day-to-day operations and management of the L&D function is organized and guided to ensure consistency with the strategies of its key, critical Stakeholders. This includes planning both operations and budgets and updating them on an annual, quarterly, and monthly cycle; or whenever it's needed.

This system and its processes plan, track, and account for the investments in L&D content that are required to support the strategic, high-payback needs of the Enterprise. This system and its processes also routinely readjust to their dynamic situation as the needs and situation of the Enterprise dictate.

The following Processes of that System will be reviewed next:

- Annual Operations Planning and Budgeting Processes
- Quarterly Operations Planning and Budgeting

Updates Processes
- Forecasting and Accounting Processes

Let's look at the first of these.

Annual Operations Planning and Budgeting Processes

Processes Purpose

The Annual Operations Planning and Budgeting Processes plans for and allocates the resources that the Enterprise has partitioned to the L&D system in a manner consistent with the strategic and short term needs of both the Enterprise and the L&D system itself.

Processes Description

The Annual Operations Planning and Budgeting Processes allocate its constrained, limited resources to its current targets. Those targets include projects for its customers, as well as projects for its internal processes and infrastructure development or improvement projects.

If the L&D system is not undertaking efforts to meet its own strategic needs – for example, conducting L&D-related research and development or eliminating its own current shortfalls, or one day it will not be "at the ready" to assist the high-performing organization in meeting the knowledge and skill needs of the critical human assets.

The Annual Operations Planning and Budgeting Processes must be built using reality-based estimates from prior experiences.

Using pretend, aggressive estimates in the desire to drive down costs or cycle times, without any real experience, needs to be recognized for what it is. That approach/philosophy only drives a need for a backup plan in case the "blue-sky plans" need to be adjusted back to reality.

It's no good running out of resources midway through the year, forcing drastic plan changes and dropping some efforts altogether due to unrealistic numbers and unrealistic plans that are "discovered" too late.

The Annual Operations Planning and Budgeting Processes interfaces with many of the other L&D systems' processes. It gets input from the Strategic Planning System and the L&D Governance and Advisory System. It provides plans (marching orders) and budgets (funding authorization or actual funds/assets) to all of the other L&D systems in order to carry out the current operational plan. These will be updated as needed by the other two processes within this system.

Are Your Annual Operations Processes Broken? Clues and Cues

Your Annual Operations Planning and Budgeting Processes may be broken if:

- You don't have an annual plan tied to specific projects and efforts.
- You never have the right amount of human, environmental, and financial resources necessary for getting the high-priority demand/must-do projects completed in a timely, quality fashion.
- Forecasted project costs, schedules, and returns on investments are seldom accurate.

Processes Summary

The Annual Operations Planning and Budgeting Processes are intended to ensure that you are knowledgeable, in sync, and in control of the investments being made with the shareholders' equity, in conformance with the priority needs of the Enterprise.

Hopefully, your L&D system already has a great deal of the planning and budgeting processes in place.

Next, we will look at the Operations Planning and Budgeting updates that should be examined quarterly – or as otherwise needed by your specific circumstances.

Quarterly Operations Planning and Budgeting Updates Processes

Processes Purpose

The Quarterly Operations Planning and Budgeting Updates Processes systematically re-examines and reallocates the L&D resources, consistent with the ever-changing strategic and tactical needs of both the Enterprise and the L&D system itself.

Processes Description

The Quarterly Operations Planning and Budgeting Updates Processes are an adjustment process typically required to provide plans and financial data to other Enterprise financial systems, operational management systems, etc.

The frequency of updates to the plans and budget allocations will be required at a pace unique to each Enterprise's current cycles.

If the L&D system is not undertaking efforts to keep pace with and understand the implications of the inevitable changes and challenges that the Stakeholder organizations will surely face, it will fall short in providing the knowledge/skill development required.

Let no one in L&D safely assume that the needs and plans of itself or the Enterprise are "that sure" for "that long."

If you believe – that the only constant today is constant change – then you should work to anticipate that change better.

Quarterly might be too seldom in some high-tech, fast-paced industries and too often for others. Your situation and business culture will dictate a pace sufficient and/or tolerable.

The Quarterly Operations Planning and Budgeting Updates Processes interface with many of the other L&D systems' processes to continuously realign with "what's happening now." The Governance and Advisory System is a key driver, but additional inputs may come from each and every other L&D system in place that enable the Curriculum Manager's Areas of Performance capabilities.

Are Your Quarterly Operations Planning and Budgeting Updates Processes Broken? Clues and Cues

Your Quarterly Operations Planning and Budgeting Updates Processes may be broken if:

- You can't tell quarter by quarter how well you will do in meeting the project goals with the necessary resources.
- The shifting needs of the Enterprise and the tradeoff decisions between projects aren't being

made (if there are not enough resources to allocate in a timely manner).

Processes Summary

The Quarterly Operations Planning and Budgeting Updates Processes keep everyone abreast of the current status of projects and resource consumption, so that if "push comes to shove" and not everything can be addressed, the critical, weighted, strategic needs of the Enterprise are driving the reallocation decisions.

Next are the Processes for forecasting and accounting.

Forecasting and Accounting Processes

Processes Purpose

The Forecasting and Accounting Processes tracks all of the expenditures and the contractual/ planned commitments to ensure that the price tags for all of the current and planned efforts are known before all of the invoices arrive.

Processes Description

The Forecasting and Accounting Processes tracks and reports all of the expenditures and allows the L&D system to be in a position to declare its ability to "give back" if asked to "give back" resources at the end of the third quarter or whenever things get too tight.

This system clearly understands where its financial obligations stand contractually. It understands the implications of the Enterprise headquarters' requests to not spend it all, but to give a portion of it back so that it might fall straight back to the bottom line and improve the financial view of the Enterprise.

After all, "a dollar not spent is a dollar back on the bottom line!"

That is a notion for the L&D community to demonstratively reflect in all of their communications to their marketplace Stakeholders – and their actions. Walk that talk about cost avoidance where appropriate, and worthy investments where determined.

The *corollary,* however, is that a dollar not invested is a greater return deferred or foregone.

If the L&D system has contractual obligations, it may or may not be in a position to give back any funds to management if requested. It had better understand its financial/contractual situation in an ongoing manner.

Are Your Forecasting and Accounting Processes Broken? Clues and Cues

Your Forecasting and Accounting Processes may be broken if:

- You don't know where you stand at all times and for all current projects in regard to your project and financial status and your project continuation/completion financial obligations.

Processes Summary

The Forecasting and Accounting Processes keeps financial score of the L&D system. You should know where you are project by project in terms of completion status, both time-wise and cost-wise.

AoP Summary

The Operations Planning Area of Performance is about your annual plan and budget that needs to be consistent with your current work needs and your longer-term work needs – and the resources you need – or will be given.

The formal Systems and Processes for addressing the Curriculum Manager's responsibilities include

- Annual Operations Planning and Budgeting Processes
- Quarterly Operations Planning and Budgeting Updates Processes
- Forecasting and Accounting Processes

Part of your responsibility as a Curriculum Manager is to adopt and/ or adapt what has been presented here for your own context. Hopefully this has provided you with some guidance for doing that.

How Are You Currently Performing This Area of Performance Competence?

Regarding the Operations Planning Area of Performance…

How are you currently **Planning this Work** – how are you deciding what needs to get done, and by whom, and when?

What, if anything, needs to change?

How are you currently **Assigning this Work** – and how are you communicating the expectations of the work assignment?

What, if anything, needs to change?

How are you currently **Monitoring the Work** – how are you focusing on the follow up monitoring of work processes and work products to insure that everything is okay?

What, if anything, needs to change?

How are you currently **Troubleshooting the Work** – how are you conducting the follow up for any of the work products or work processes where you spotted discrepancies, in order to resolve them?

What, if anything, needs to change?

Chapter Summary & Transition

This chapter was intended to address the Operations Planning Area of Performance responsibilities of a Curriculum Manager – where you determine your annual budget consistent with your Strategic Plans and the current needs of your Customers and other Stakeholders.

This chapter logically leads to the next, but your needs may cause you to want to skip around.

The list of chapters and their pages numbers are presented next for your personal navigation needs and desires.

1	What Does a Curriculum Manager Do?	1

2	AoP: Stakeholder Needs Assessment & Alignment	27
3	AoP: Strategic Planning & Management	53
4	AoP: Operations Planning & Management	65
5	AoP: Results Measurement	79
6	AoP: Improvement Planning	95
7	AoP: Communications	107
8	AoP: Product & Service Line Design	120
9	AoP: Product & Service Line Development	143
10	AoP: Product & Service Line Deployment	169
11	AoP: Process Design & Redesign	193
12	AoP: Human Assets	203
13	AoP: Environmental Assets	222
14	AoP: Special Assignments	241
15	Summary & Close	247
16	Additional Related Resources & References	254

Suggested Chapter Reflection & Reaction

I would suggest that prior to jumping into whichever chapter meets your needs that you give pause for a moment to reflect on the following and make some notes:

- What are your own "ah-ha's" so far?

- Are your Operations Planning Systems and Processes Adequate to your needs? If not, what is the cost of the problem or opportunity, and what are the potential Returns for any Investments for improving these?

- How would you need to think about this model differently than it is presented?

- What language changes and deletions or additions might you need to make?

- What are all of the implications for you and your L&D function thus far?

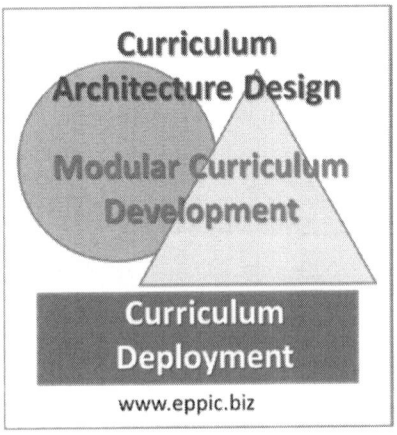

At the Core of a Curriculum Manager's
Performance Competence Requirements
are the architecture, development and deployment of
performance-enabling
Instructional and Informational Content

5 - AREA OF PERFORMANCE: RESULTS MEASUREMENT

Chapter Overview

Read or scan this chapter if you are concerned with:

- **Results Measurement** - establishing meaningful metrics, measures and measurement mechanisms for gathering, manipulating and reporting data/information to all Stakeholders

This chapter is intended to provide you with some details related to this Area of Performance (AoP).

L4- Results Measurement is where the metrics systems are put into place and then operated to establish the scorecard data gathering and reporting systems, and then reports out the data.

As you read through this chapter keep in mind your potential need to adapt this content to your context – or to adapt your context to this content.

This chapter fits within the overall flow of the model as presented in the following graphic.

Curriculum Manager's Areas of Performance Competence Model

LEADERSHIP AoPs - Planning & Management
- Stakeholder Needs Assessment & Alignment
- Strategic Planning
- Operations Planning
- Results Measurement
- Improvement Planning
- Communications

CORE AoPs - Planning & Management
- Product & Service Line Design
- Product & Service Line Development
- Product & Service Line Deployment

SUPPORT AoPs - Planning & Management
- Process Design and Redesign
- Human Assets
- Environmental Assets
- Special Assignments

Adapted from the Management Areas of Performance Model
©2002 Guy W. Wallace

AoP: L4- Results Measurement

Overview

This system measures and reports the metrics of the L&D system. It turns data into information and interprets and reports it to the Enterprise leadership, staff, and its key customers and Stakeholders.

This system pulls data from everywhere in the L&D system and reports it back to all of its constituencies, appropriate to each audience and their specific needs.

AoP Overview

The **Results Measurement** Area of Performance involves developing a plan for implementing/updating a results measurement (Balanced Scorecard-*like*) system. The intent is to put into place a system of data gathering, manipulations and reports to allow for monitoring the performance of the unit, and troubleshooting any problems that are discerned.

Typical AoP Outputs

The Curriculum Manager's **"outputs"** of this Area of Performance typically include:

- Results Measurement Plans
- Results Reports

Typical AoP Tasks

The "**tasks**" of this Area of Performance, related to the outputs above, typically include:

- Developing a Results Measurement plan draft
- Reviewing the plan with your management, and subordinates
- Updating the Results Measurement per the feedback received
- Communicating the final plan with specific messages to the appropriate group(s) through the appropriate channel(s)
- Following the plan, monitoring other implementation, and adjusting/updating it as necessary

AoP Systems & Processes Overview
Next we will look at a formal System for addressing this AoP:

- **Results Measurement System**

The following four Processes of that System will be reviewed next:

- Cost/Benefits Measurement System Design and Deployment Processes
- Ongoing Cost/Benefits Measurement and Feedback Receiving Processes
- L&D Project Lessons Learned Processes
- Results Reporting and Archiving Processes

Let's look at the first of these.

Cost/Benefits Measurement System Design and Deployment Processes

Processes Purpose

The Cost/Benefits Measurement System Design and Deployment Processes create, deploy, and maintain the measurement system and mechanism(s) for all of L&D. It's a type of "balanced scorecard" (BSC).

Processes Description

The Cost/Benefits Measurement System Design and Deployment Processes create a measurement system and a plan and process to deploy that mechanism. A decision will need to be made whether or not to measure each new product or service, as well as whether or not to measure each new internal process or infrastructure improvement effort.

Addressing these (or not) should be a conscious business decision. It should be a decision made with an eye toward the return on investment, because there will always be a cost involved for any effort at measurement. Before being gathered, it should be clear *why* the data is being gathered and *how* it will be used.

After it's been up and running for a while, this process will need to be continuously improved and perhaps pruned.

The measurement mechanism(s) for each new product and/or service must be considered in terms of the value for cost of obtaining the data.

The exactness of the data required needs to be determined on a case-by-case basis. The amount of data and the extent and cost of the effort to capture the data needs to be determined. The statistical accuracy requirements of the data need to be accounted for in the measurement plan.

The results of the other elements of the entire L&D system, such as the cost/benefits of the Governance and Advisory System, need to be tracked, along with many other systems and process efforts.

Are Your Cost/Benefits Measurement System Design and Deployment Processes Broken? Clues and Cues

Your Cost/Benefits Measurement System Design and Deployment Processes may be broken if:

- You don't measure or plan to measure key L&D efforts.
- There is not a systematic business approach used to decide which efforts get measured and which do not.
- Measurement is inconsistent, labor intensive, and the results reported are not insightful.
- You rarely or never measure learning, performance, and/or business results.

Processes Summary

The Cost/Benefits Measurement System Design and Deployment Processes need to create a meaningful measurement system and a plan and process for both developing and deploying that mechanism.

Next are the Processes for ongoing cost/benefits measurement and feedback.

Ongoing Cost/Benefits Measurement and Feedback Receiving Processes

Processes Purpose

The Ongoing Cost/Benefits Measurement and Feedback Receiving Processes capture the data from the Cost/Benefits Measurement System Design and Deployment Processes Cost/Benefits Measurement System, packages it, and reports it out to the appropriate parties within the Enterprise.

Processes Description

The Ongoing Cost/Benefits Measurement and Feedback Receiving Processes measures all Cost/Benefits Measurement System Design and Deployment Processes efforts and results, including similar measures of impact as in Kirkpatrick's four levels of evaluation for Cost/Benefits Measurement System Design and Deployment Processes and more!

Kirkpatrick's four levels of evaluation require that measurement effort be expended to assess both the costs incurred as well as the results obtained for the Cost/Benefits Measurement System Design and Deployment Processes products.

The four levels of evaluation measurement are, in my wording, the following:

- **Satisfaction** (Level 1) – Whether or not the Target Audiences were satisfied with the product
- **Mastery** (Level 2) – Whether or not learning objectives were mastered
- **Transfer** (Level 3) – Whether what was supposed to be mastered was taken back and used on the job

- **Return on Investment** (Level 4) – The return on investment for the effort and expense (Results in business terms)

L&D can be measured in many manners from the impact of an individual product of L&D, to the impact of an entire set of curricula, to the overall impact of customer and other Stakeholder satisfaction measures, return on investment, and economic value add.

This system creates an open communications channel into the L&D system for any and all cost/benefit feedback or other related inputs and inquiries from its customers and Stakeholders.

Are Your Ongoing Cost/Benefits Measurement and Feedback Receiving Processes Broken? Clues and Cues

Your Ongoing Cost/Benefits Measurement and Feedback Receiving Processes may be broken if:

- You don't know your general or specific costs, satisfaction levels for any or all of your Stakeholders, mastery levels of learners after training, transfer levels back to the job, and return on investment for any or all of your critical L&D efforts.
- You initially collected data, but efforts to do it have declined over time.

Processes Summary

The Ongoing Cost/Benefits Measurement and Feedback Receiving Processes are necessary to measure the health of L&D and its products and services, and any or all internal project efforts for L&D process or infrastructure improvements.

Next, we will look at the processes for L&D project lessons learned.

L&D Project Lessons Learned Processes

Processes Purpose

The L&D Project Lessons Learned Processes capture data unique to the internal *lessons learned* by the participants within L&D processes regarding their experiences in using or being a part of the process.

Processes Description

The L&D Project Lessons Learned Processes capture mostly nonfinancial data. This system gathers feedback from all of the participants engaged in the L&D system, such as customers, suppliers, or other Stakeholders.

Feedback is the lifeblood of continuous improvement.

Lessons Learned are intended to share what works and under what conditions, as well as what doesn't work under what conditions, for the purpose of continuously improving the processes.

Each Stakeholder has a stake in either the processes themselves or in the results of the processes. Their needs vary. There may be conflicting requirements among the varied Stakeholders. Each needs to be balanced and weighed to assess which requirements will win in the inevitable conflicts that arise.

Are Your Project Lessons Learned Processes Broken? Clues and Cues

Your Project Lessons Learned Processes may be broken if:

- You keep seeing the same kinds of mistakes and ineffective, costly approaches being used over and over again in successive projects.
- Your team doesn't know what worked and what didn't work in the past, or why.

Processes Summary

The L&D Project Lessons Learned Processes provide best practices and lessons learned from specific projects, in an attempt to help others deal with similar issues and avoid common problems.

Next, we'll look at the process for reporting and archiving results.

Results Reporting and Archiving Processes

Processes Purpose

The Results Reporting and Archiving Processes gather all of the L&D results data, manipulate the data into an intelligent and understandable information format, and then reports it to Stakeholders appropriate to their needs. It also archives it for future reference.

Processes Description

The most appropriate tool to use to report results is something similar to the balanced scorecard. The measurement philosophy to avoid is the "butts in seats" or "butts on sites" (Web sites) numbers.

These numbers may have some value, but they don't adequately assess what is needed to better understand the return on investment and economic value add potential of human capital development investments.

Gathering data and reporting it can occur in different cycles. Project data can be gathered throughout the project period or after the fact.

Issues will arise regarding data timeliness and quality versus costs and inconveniences. Understanding exactly what, where, and when decisions will be made using such data can lead to better and more efficient plans for gathering data and reporting it.

Are Your Results Reporting and Archiving Processes Broken? Clues and Cues

Your Results Reporting and Archiving Processes may be broken if:

- Your Stakeholders don't know the results of the investments and expenses made in Enterprise L&D.
- You can't really begin to predict the future in terms of L&D costs and returns based on past L&D projects/efforts.
- You can't go back and look at or find past project results.

Processes Summary

The Results Reporting and Archiving Processes reports what happened, when and where, to Stakeholder groups in order to better meet their needs. Some have simple interest needs to be met, while others have due diligence and fiduciary/ financial responsibilities to the Enterprise and the Enterprise shareholders/owners.

If "what gets measured gets attention," then the L&D system's Governance and Advisory System needs to put in place the mechanisms to gather, report, and archive meaningful data. Then the L&D Governance and Advisory groups and L&D leadership need to act on that data.

AoP Summary

This **Results Measurement** Area of Performance is about measuring and reporting results.

The formal Systems and four Processes for addressing the Curriculum Manager's responsibilities include:

- Cost/Benefits Measurement System Design and Deployment Processes
- Ongoing Cost/Benefits Measurement and Feedback Receiving Processes
- L&D Project Lessons Learned Processes
- Results Reporting and Archiving Processes

Part of your responsibility as a Curriculum Manager is to adopt and/ or adapt what has been presented here for your own context. Hopefully this has provided you with some guidance for doing that.

How Are You Currently Performing This Area of Performance Competence?

Regarding this Results Measurement Area of Performance...

How are you currently **Planning this Work** – and how are you deciding what needs to get done, and by whom, and when?

What, if anything, needs to change?

How are you currently **Assigning this Work** – and how are you communicating the expectations of the work assignment?

What, if anything, needs to change?

How are you currently **Monitoring this Work** – and how are you focusing on the follow up monitoring of work processes and work products to insure that everything is okay?

What, if anything, needs to change?

How are you currently **Troubleshooting this Work** – and how are you following up for any of the work products or work processes where you spotted discrepancies, in order to resolve them?

What, if anything, needs to change?

Chapter Summary & Transition

This chapter was intended to address Results Measurement – where you measure and report out the results, using business metrics for the results of your investments.

This chapter logically leads to the next, but your needs may cause you to want to skip around.

The list of chapters and their pages numbers are presented next for your personal navigation needs and desires.

1	What Does a Curriculum Manager Do?	1
2	AoP: Stakeholder Needs Assessment & Alignment	27
3	AoP: Strategic Planning & Management	53
4	AoP: Operations Planning & Management	65
5	AoP: Results Measurement	79
6	AoP: Improvement Planning	95
7	AoP: Communications	107
8	AoP: Product & Service Line Design	120
9	AoP: Product & Service Line Development	143
10	AoP: Product & Service Line Deployment	169
11	AoP: Process Design & Redesign	193
12	AoP: Human Assets	203
13	AoP: Environmental Assets	222
14	AoP: Special Assignments	241
15	Summary & Close	247
16	Additional Related Resources & References	254

Suggested Chapter Reflection & Reaction

I would suggest that prior to jumping into whichever chapter meets your needs that you give pause for a moment to reflect on the following and make some notes:

- What are your own "ah-ha's" so far?

- Is your Results Measurement System and Processes adequate to your needs? If not, what is the cost of the problem or opportunity, and what are the potential Returns for any Investments for improving these?

- How would you need to think about this model differently than it is presented?

- What language changes and deletions or additions might you need to make?

- What are all of the implications for you and your L&D function thus far?

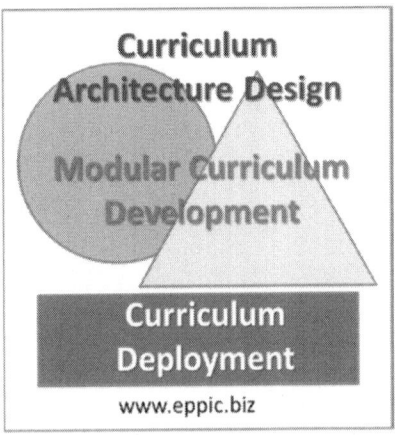

At the Core of a Curriculum Manager's
Performance Competence Requirements
are the architecture, development and deployment of
performance-enabling
Instructional and Informational Content

6 - AREA OF PERFORMANCE: IMPROVEMENT PLANNING

Chapter Overview

Read or scan this chapter if you are concerned with:

- **Improvement Planning** - systematically improving internal processes for ROI benefit, and for achieving the annual operational and long-term strategic goals and plans

This chapter is intended to provide you with some details related to this AoP, including a formal System and Processes for accomplishing the Curriculum Manager's responsibilities for this Area of Performance.

L5- Improvement Planning - is where improvements within the L&D function, and/or its supply chains, are planned to maximize returns and reduced risk – where warranted.

This chapter fits within the overall flow of the model as presented in the following graphic.

Curriculum Manager's Areas of Performance Competence Model

LEADERSHIP AoPs - Planning & Management
- Stakeholder Needs Assessment & Alignment
- Strategic Planning
- Operations Planning
- Results Measurement
- Improvement Planning
- Communications

CORE AoPs - Planning & Management
- Product & Service Line Design
- Product & Service Line Development
- Product & Service Line Deployment

SUPPORT AoPs - Planning & Management
- Process Design and Redesign
- Human Assets
- Environmental Assets
- Special Assignments

Adapted from the Management Areas of Performance Model
©2002 Guy W. Wallace

As you read through this chapter keep in mind your potential need to adapt this content to your context – or to adapt your context to this content.

AoP: L5- Improvement Planning

AoP Overview

The **Improvement Planning** Area of Performance involves developing plans for improving internal processes where the potential, forecasted ROI exceeds the internal "hurdle rates" expected by the Enterprise, consistent with the goals of achieving the annual operational plan objectives and the long-term strategic goals and objectives of the Enterprise.

Typical AoP Outputs

The Curriculum Manager "**outputs**" of this Area of Performance typically include

- Improvement Plans

Typical AoP Tasks

The "**tasks**" of this Area of Performance, related to the outputs above, typically include

- Developing an Improvement plan draft
- Reviewing the Improvement plan with your management, and subordinates
- Updating the Improvement plan per the feedback received
- Communicating the final Improvement plan with specific group(s) through the appropriate channel(s)

- Following the Improvement plan, monitoring implementation and successes/failures, and adjusting/updating the Improvement plan as necessary

AoP Systems & Processes Overview

Next we will look at a formal System for addressing this AoP:

- **Improvement Planning System**

In order to better use the shareholders' equity, process improvement must focus on high-payback areas consistent with the L&D objectives and the direction from the Governance and Advisory System.

This system is responsible for improving L&D's own systems and processes in response to issues and trends uncovered by the measurement system.

This system also provides structure and order to the quality and process improvement efforts for both incremental, continuous improvement, and radical, discontinuous improvement to L&D processes, including the systems and processes that provide the human and environmental assets required by those processes.

This system's processes organize the quality/process improvement efforts for both continuous improvement and discontinuous improvement of the L&D systems and processes.

The following Processes of this System will be reviewed next:

- L&D Issues Generation and Assessment Processes

- L&D Improvement Project Planning and Management Processes

Let's look at the first of these.

L&D Issues Generation and Assessment Processes

Processes Purpose

The L&D Issues Generation and Assessment Processes identify both L&D's current and future issues (high-payback problems/opportunities) and bring them to the attention of the Governance and Advisory System.

Processes Description

The L&D Issues Generation and Assessment Processes identify things to work on within the L&D system: either problems and/or opportunities. It validates and "costs out" the problem/opportunity and better forecasts return on investment and economic value add for any improvement effort.

The systems and mechanisms for initially gathering this data might include the balanced scorecard, suggestion boxes, E-mail, or other complaint systems, and/or polling of the various Enterprise leaders and employees participating within each of the L&D systems' many processes.

Regardless of the source of initial insight regarding the L&D systems' shortcomings and missed (current or future) opportunities, they will need to be validated.

The validation processes might be similar to most Enterprises' quality or problem-solving methods. The problems'/opportunities' cost of nonconformance can be determined as well as the cost of conformance to determine ROI potential.

The cost of conformance can be estimated based on rough plans and prior experience activities for addressing other, similarly scoped projects.

Are Your Issues Generation and Assessment Processes Broken? Clues and Cues

The L&D Issues Generation and Assessment Processes may be broken if:

- Significant L&D system problems and opportunities are not determined, validated, or addressed in a rational, systematic manner.
- Major L&D problems that aren't addressed incur avoidable, recurring costs that reach a level of significance and/or intolerance that detracts from the key business focus of the L&D system.

Processes Summary

The L&D Issues Generation and Assessment Processes ensure that rational steps are taken to implement improvements in the L&D system.

The data, not opinions, should inform and rule resourcing decisions made inside the L&D system.

Next are the L&D Improvement Project Planning and Management Processes.

Improvement Project Planning and Management Processes

Processes Purpose

The L&D Improvement Project Planning and Management Processes takes the validated problems/opportunities and plans a project to address the needs and then oversees the improvement initiative efforts, much as any other major/minor improvement initiative.

Processes Description

The L&D Improvement Project Planning and Management Processes are much like any other project planning effort. This process practices good project management and gets the job done.

Using best project management practices appropriate to the size, scope, and impact of the project's anticipated results, the improvement project proceeds as guided by the project's management/governance structure.

Are Your Improvement Project Planning and Management Processes Broken? Clues and Cues

The L&D Improvement Project Planning and Management Processes may be broken if:

- Improvement initiatives are undertaken without a clear plan of tasks, responsibilities, schedule, or costs.

- Improvement initiatives are routinely poorly conceived, behind schedule, or over budget.
- Improvement initiatives are not considered "true projects" with expectations for results, resources, communication, etc., equivalent to "client work."
- Projects drift and seem uncontrolled despite a well-documented plan.
- None of the really big problems are being fixed.

Processes Summary

The L&D Improvement Project Planning and Management Processes rationally plans improvement initiatives much as any major or minor initiative planning effort, and manages the project job per the plan or adjusted as the situation dictates.

AoP Summary

This **Improvement Planning** Area of Performance is about improving those processes within your sphere of control as a Curriculum Manager.

The formal **Improvement Planning** System's Processes for addressing the Curriculum Manager's responsibilities include:

- L&D Issues Generation and Assessment Processes
- L&D Improvement Project Planning and Management Processes

Part of your responsibility as a Curriculum Manager is to adopt and/ or adapt what has been presented here for your own context. Hopefully this has provided you with some guidance for doing that.

How Are You Currently Performing This Area of Performance Competence?

Regarding the Improvement Planning Area of Performance…

How are you currently **Planning this Work** – and how are you deciding what needs to get done, and by whom, and when?

What, if anything, needs to change?

How are you currently **Assigning this Work** – and how are you communicating the expectations of the work assignment?

What, if anything, needs to change?

How are you currently **Monitoring this Work** – and how are you focusing on the follow up monitoring of work processes and work products to insure that everything is okay?

What, if anything, needs to change?

How are you currently **Troubleshooting Work** – and how are you following up for any work products or work processes where you spotted discrepancies, in order to resolve them?

What, if anything, needs to change?

Chapter Summary & Transition

This chapter was intended to address **Improvement Planning** – where you improve your own processes.

The L&D Processes Improvement System and Processes ensure that worthy improvement needs are uncovered/discovered, and that they are addressed methodically and rationally, using the best practices of process improvement and good project management.

This chapter logically leads to the next, but your needs may cause you to want to skip around.

The list of chapters and their pages numbers are presented next for your personal navigation needs and desires.

1	What Does a Curriculum Manager Do?	1
2	AoP: Stakeholder Needs Assessment & Alignment	27
3	AoP: Strategic Planning & Management	53
4	AoP: Operations Planning & Management	65
5	AoP: Results Measurement	79
6	AoP: Improvement Planning	95
7	AoP: Communications	107
8	AoP: Product & Service Line Design	120
9	AoP: Product & Service Line Development	143
10	AoP: Product & Service Line Deployment	169
11	AoP: Process Design & Redesign	193

12	AoP: Human Assets	203
13	AoP: Environmental Assets	222
14	AoP: Special Assignments	241
15	Summary & Close	247
16	Additional Related Resources & References	254

Suggested Chapter Reflection & Reaction

I would suggest that prior to jumping into whichever chapter meets your needs that you give pause for a moment to reflect on the following and make some notes:

- What are your own "ah-ha's" so far?

- Are your Improvement Planning Processes adequate to your needs? If not, what is the cost of the problem or opportunity, and what are the potential Returns for any Investments for improving these?

- How would you need to think about this model differently than it is presented?

- What language changes and deletions or additions might you need to make?

- What are all of the implications for you and your L&D function thus far?

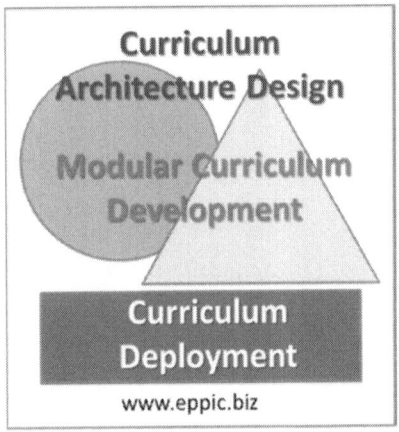

At the Core of a Curriculum Manager's
Performance Competence Requirements
are the architecture, development and deployment of
performance-enabling
Instructional and Informational Content

7 - AREA OF PERFORMANCE: COMMUNICATIONS

Chapter Overview

Read or scan this chapter if you are concerned with:

- **Communications** – assessing your Customers, other Stakeholders as communications target audiences, and determining their needs; and then planning and managing all of the one-way and two-way communications – both proactively and reactively needed, for both internal and external audiences.

This chapter is intended to provide you with some details related to this Area of Performance, including some formal Processes that you might need to have in place.

L6- Communications Planning & Management is where the communications messages and mechanisms are provided for in order to reach all Enterprise-wide and external audiences – as appropriate to your role as a Curriculum Manager.

This chapter fits within the overall flow of the model as presented in the following graphic.

Curriculum Manager's Areas of Performance Competence Model

LEADERSHIP AoPs - Planning & Management
- Stakeholder Needs Assessment & Alignment
- Strategic Planning
- Operations Planning
- Results Measurement
- Improvement Planning
- Communications

CORE AoPs - Planning & Management
- Product & Service Line Design
- Product & Service Line Development
- Product & Service Line Deployment

SUPPORT AoPs - Planning & Management
- Process Design and Redesign
- Human Assets
- Environmental Assets
- Special Assignments

Adapted from the Management Areas of Performance Model
©2002 Guy W. Wallace

As you read through this chapter keep in mind your potential need to adapt this content to your context – or to adapt your context to this content.

AoP: L6- Communications

AoP Overview

The **Communications** Area of Performance involves developing a plan for communications to all Stakeholders. The intent is to put into place a system of routine and non-routine communications.

Typical Outputs

The Curriculum Manager's "**outputs**" for this Area of Performance typically include

- Communications Plan that addresses each appropriate Target Audience segment and their routine and proactive communications, as well as any likely, potential, non-routine and reactive communications.

Typical Tasks

The "**tasks**" of this Area of Performance, related to the outputs above, typically include:

- Determining the Target Audiences for Communications from you and your team

- Developing a Communications plan draft

- Reviewing the plan with your management, subordinates and Stakeholders

- Updating the Communications plan per the feedback received

- Communicating the final Communications plan with specific group(s) through the appropriate channel(s)

- Following the Communications plan, monitoring implementation and successes/failures, and adjusting/updating the Communications plan as necessary

AoP Systems & Processes Overview

Next we will look at a formal System for addressing this AoP:

- **Communications System**

The following Processes of this System will be reviewed next:

- Stakeholder Communications Processes

Let's look at the first of these.

L&D Stakeholder Communications Processes

Processes Purpose

The L&D Stakeholder Communications Processes determines exactly who the L&D system's Stakeholders are and what their needs for information are and it delivers information and data to each Stakeholder group via the most efficient communication channels.

Processes Description

In the L&D Stakeholder Communications Processes, Stakeholders vary by the type of organization the Enterprise is and its marketplace.

- **Government** – This Stakeholder group wins all disputes and conflicts of opinions under the laws of its jurisdiction and domain, and it decides issues of both compliance and penalties.

    The Curriculum Manager needs to determine their responsibilities and the data required for communicating with the Stakeholder Groups within this category.

- **Shareholders/Owners** – This Stakeholder group can always sell out or take their money (sell their shares) and invest elsewhere. If the Enterprise is not meeting their financial targets for growth and returns, they can remove their money from this concern and place their bets elsewhere.

The Curriculum Manager needs to determine their responsibilities and the data required for communicating with the Stakeholder Groups within this category.

- **Board of Directors** – This group of Stakeholders is the elected representatives of the owners/shareholders and have a special fiduciary responsibility to the owners. They develop strategies and tactics and oversee the development and deployment of policies and procedures consistent with strategy.

    The Curriculum Manager needs to determine their

responsibilities and the data required for communicating with the Stakeholder Groups within this category.

- **Executives** – This group of Stakeholders is hired to strategize, plan, and manage the overall direction of the Enterprise. They hire and fire managers to conduct daily operations consistent with the business plans, strategies, and tactics the board approved, and they provide the necessary resources and funds.

  The Curriculum Manager needs to determine their responsibilities and the data required for communicating with the Stakeholder Groups within this category.

- **Management** – These are the managers, supervisors, and leads of the targeted learners (at all levels).

  The Curriculum Manager needs to determine their responsibilities and the data required for communicating with the Stakeholder Groups within this category.

- **Customers** – These are the internal and sometimes external Learners: the participants and users of the L&D, Content.

  The Curriculum Manager needs to determine their responsibilities and the data required for communicating with the Stakeholder Groups within this category.

- **Employees** – These are the staff members of the L&D organization.

  The Curriculum Manager needs to determine their responsibilities and the data required for communicating with the Stakeholder Groups within this category.

- **Suppliers** – These are the external and internal suppliers who support the L&D processes and provide inputs, task performance, and/or deal with outputs. They could include team members from within the Enterprise, caterers, material suppliers, consultants, and contractors.

  The Curriculum Manager needs to determine their responsibilities and the data required for communicating with the Stakeholder Groups within this category.

- **Communities** – This can include formal or informal groups such as professional societies, street pickets, industry standards groups, and family members.

  The Curriculum Manager needs to determine their responsibilities and the data required for communicating with the Stakeholder Groups within this category.

The L&D Stakeholder Communications Processes ensures that the Customers and Stakeholders of Enterprise L&D, including the potential learners to be served.

Are Your Stakeholder Communications Processes Broken? Clues and Cues

Your L&D Stakeholder Communications Processes may be broken if:

- Stakeholder groups have had to ask for information that is really viewed as "needed to know" by both of them and by the L&D Governance and Advisory groups.
- Stakeholders complain about the lack of information available.
- Frequently asked questions are not being captured, and then the answers proactively "pushed" out to like audiences.
- Surveys discover that L&D Target Audiences and other Stakeholder groups do not understand what's available and how to access it or participate in it.

Processes Summary

The L&D Stakeholder Communications Processes are intended to ensure that information is available to those who want to access ("pull") it and/or is proactively deployed ("pushed") to those critical audiences who need it.

AoP Summary

This Area of Performance is about determining who to formally communicate with as a Curriculum Manager.

The formal System's Processes for addressing the Curriculum Manager's responsibilities include the

- Stakeholder Communications Processes

Part of your responsibility as a Curriculum Manager is to adopt and/ or adapt what has been presented here for your own context. Hopefully this has provided you with some guidance for doing that.

How Are You Currently Performing This Area of Performance Competence?

Regarding the Communications Area of Performance…

How are you currently **Planning this Work** – and how are you deciding what needs to get done, and by whom, and when?

What, if anything, needs to change?

How are you currently **Assigning this Work** – and how are you communicating the expectations of the work assignment?

What, if anything, needs to change?

How are you currently **Monitoring this Work** – and how are you focusing on the follow up monitoring of work processes and work products to insure that everything is okay?

What, if anything, needs to change?

How are you currently **Troubleshooting this Work** – and how are you following up for any of the work products or work processes where you spotted discrepancies, in order to resolve them?

What, if anything, needs to change?

Chapter Summary & Transition

This chapter was intended to address Communications Area of Performance responsibilities of your role as a Curriculum Manager.

This chapter logically leads to the next, but your needs may cause you to want to skip around.

The list of chapters and their pages numbers are presented next for your personal navigation needs and desires.

1	What Does a Curriculum Manager Do?	1
2	AoP: Stakeholder Needs Assessment & Alignment	27
3	AoP: Strategic Planning & Management	53
4	AoP: Operations Planning & Management	65
5	AoP: Results Measurement	79
6	AoP: Improvement Planning	95
7	AoP: Communications	107
8	AoP: Product & Service Line Design	120
9	AoP: Product & Service Line Development	143
10	AoP: Product & Service Line Deployment	169
11	AoP: Process Design & Redesign	193
12	AoP: Human Assets	203

13	AoP: Environmental Assets	222
14	AoP: Special Assignments	241
15	Summary & Close	247
16	Additional Related Resources & References	254

Suggested Chapter Reflection & Reaction

I would suggest that prior to jumping into whichever chapter meets your needs that you give pause for a moment to reflect on the following and make some notes:

- What are your own "ah-ha's" so far?

- Are your Communications systems and processes adequate to the needs of all of your Stakeholders? If not, what is the cost of the problem or opportunity, and what are the potential Returns for any Investments for improving these?

- How would you need to think about this model differently than it is presented?

- What language changes and deletions or additions might you need to make?

- What are all of the implications for you and your L&D function thus far?

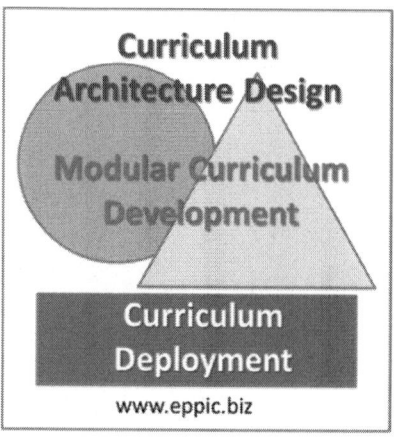

At the Core of a Curriculum Manager's
Performance Competence Requirements
are the architecture, development and deployment of
performance-enabling
Instructional and Informational Content

8 - AREA OF PERFORMANCE: PRODUCT & SERVICE LINE DESIGN

Chapter Overview

Read or scan this chapter if you are concerned with:

- **Product & Service Line Design** – which conducts the efforts to "systematically engineer" or "architect" the performance-based products and services that make sense from a performance impact perspective and an ROI perspective to your Customers and Stakeholders. This is Portfolio Management of L&D/ T&D products and services.

This chapter is intended to provide you with some details related to this Core Area of Performance (AoP) including the development of an **architectural blueprint and plan** to guide your later development efforts – really enabling rapid development without the typical gaps and overlaps that a rapid approach can inadvertently create without such a plan.

This is the first of three Core AoPs of a Curriculum Manager. **These three are the heart, the reason for being, of an L&D organization in an Enterprise.** The three Core AoPs are depicted in the following graphic.

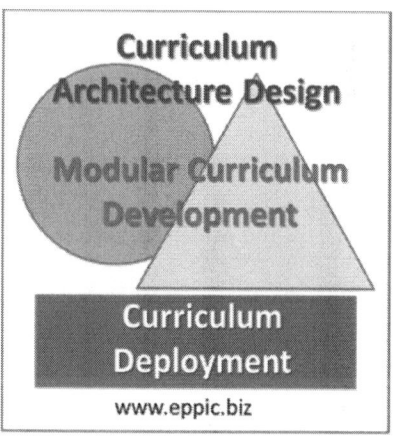

C1- Product & Service Line Design – is the first of the three Core Areas of Performance that are central to any Curriculum Manager's job.

This AoP helps to avoid L&D Content overlaps and gaps – which are very costly, both in first costs and then multiplied over and over again in life cycle costs.

This is where my **Curriculum Architecture Design – CAD** methods fit.

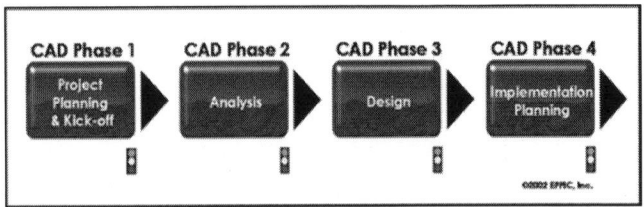

More about CAD – Curriculum Architecture Design later in this chapter.

This chapter fits within the overall flow of the model and content of this book as presented in the following graphic.

Curriculum Manager's Areas of Performance Competence Model

LEADERSHIP AoPs - Planning & Management
- ☐ Stakeholder Needs Assessment & Alignment
- ☐ Strategic Planning
- ☐ Operations Planning
- ☐ Results Measurement
- ☐ Improvement Planning
- ☐ Communications

CORE AoPs - Planning & Management
- ☐ Product & Service Line Design
- ☐ Product & Service Line Development
- ☐ Product & Service Line Deployment

SUPPORT AoPs - Planning & Management
- ☐ Process Design and Redesign
- ☐ Human Assets
- ☐ Environmental Assets
- ☐ Special Assignments

Adapted from the Management Areas of Performance Model
©2002 Guy W. Wallace

As you read through this chapter keep in mind your potential need to adapt this content to your context – or to adapt your context to this content.

AoP: C1- Product & Service Line Design

AoP Overview

There are many potential L&D targets within an Enterprise. Many are important. Few are absolutely critical. Few Enterprises are in a current state of self-actualizing and have enough time and dollars to "spray and pray" or "oil all of the squeaky wheels" when it comes to L&D.

Resources are always scarce, and there are always more problems and opportunities that you should, rather than could, address.

This Area of Performance should use a reputable ISD approach to systematically define the performance-enabling awareness, knowledge, and skills; assess any existing L&D that the shareholders have already invested in; and then architect or systems engineer the product line and the service line - if non-product "services" are also intended to be made available – for each PUSH Target Audience.

The process produces a **Curriculum Architecture Design** that includes both a product line and service line architecture – as appropriate. Product and service priorities for high-payback and critical business needs should be quickly, but carefully identified and quantified – and then resourced for development/acquisition.

Only those Enterprise needs with highest ROI impact should be addressed; and only at the appropriate time given that there might be more efforts than just "training" involved in enabling the Performance Competence requirements of the Learners/Performers.

While the final list of medium and low priorities may include someone else's highest priority, maybe even their number one priority, that does not make it right to address from an Enterprise-wide view.

Your high priorities may be numerous in count, and some may need to be conducted in an integrated, Program Management effort or a Portfolio Management manner, to be most effective and efficient.

Also, the enabling elements of any business process are more than just the human knowledge and skills required. There are other factors that cause or inhibit performance, and some L&D professionals are in a great position to help the Enterprise managers and executives see what the other gaps are, that may be critical enablers of their Enterprise processes. Those managers and executives may then guide and resource whatever non-instructional interventions are needed through those development and deployment efforts as well.

Maybe a process and a tool need to be improved, and no training is really needed at all! Or maybe both instructional and non-instructional interventions will be needed, making all projects more independent and complex.

Again, only those potential *knowledge-/skill-deficient* targets with high-payback, via increased revenues and/or reductions in costs and cycle time or that mitigate significant Enterprise risks, should be planned, resourced, and managed. Only those targets that are critically important to the Enterprise in the short and/or long term should be funded. No "low-hanging fruit" L&D projects/products should ever be addressed – no matter how large the Target Audience or "cool" the topic.

There is no reason to do otherwise from a shareholder viewpoint – no one should strategically place their bets on efforts that don't promise significant ROI. Not when resources are constrained. And when aren't they?

When the Stakeholders' bets are placed, the L&D system needs to be able to handle the complex load of projects and activities necessary. Doing so for "so-so" projects, that don't have significant returns, are more difficult because many of those who need to be involved just don't see the point. They will find better uses for their time.

AoP Typical Outputs

- A Portfolio Plan that identifies both the key PUSH Target Audiences and the current state of adequacy of their Learning Paths and content that meets their performance-driven needs directly – and a listing of all other PULL Target Audiences and a listing of available content that address their needs (less directly) might also be produced

- A L&D Path and Planning Guide for each key PUSH Target Audience - and possibly for PULL Target Audiences as well

- A list of prioritized L&D project targets for any gaps and modification efforts with ROI figures from each advisory group

- A final priority list of target projects for L&D to address

AoP Typical Tasks

- Conduct Portfolio Planning efforts for all Target Audiences

- Conduct the **Curriculum Architecture Design (CAD)** efforts – or equivalent efforts – for the key PUSH Target Audiences to define the products and service to enable these Target Audiences' Performance Competence

- Planning for post-CAD efforts for development and implementation of the critical gaps

AoP Systems & Processes Overview

Next we will look at a formal System for addressing this AoP:

- Portfolio and Curriculum Planning

The following three Processes of this System will be reviewed next:

- Product and Service Line Program Management Processes
- Product Line Design Processes
- Service Line Design Processes

Let's look at the first of these three.

Product and Service Line Program Management Processes

Processes Purpose

The Product and Service Line Program Management Processes enable the determination, across the Enterprise, which L&D Target Audiences needs are truly priorities and need to be addressed most formally.

The business decisions made as to which are the highest priorities from the various units/segments of the Enterprise and should be addressed, and in what order, are the province of the Governance and Advisory groups presented in chapter 2.

This process interacts with the Governance and Advisory System and responds, perhaps with plans covering a multi-year period, depending on the complexity of the Enterprise's needs and its ability to resource those needs.

Processes Description

The L&D Product and Service Line Program Management Processes exist to determine the sequence of projects to address specific performance-based needs, with available L&D resources based on the prioritized, critical Enterprise needs.

No Target Audience should be addressed because it's their turn. Only address those Target Audiences that are in mission-critical processes and are experiencing performance issues or are expected to have performance issues where the cost of nonconformance (CONC) is large, and the cost of conformance (COC) suggests return on investment that is sufficient compared to the Enterprise hurdle rates and other opportunities.

The CONC is equivalent to the R in ROI – and the COC is equivalent to the I in ROI. These are terms from the Quality movement.

There is no sense in spending shareholder equity, future profits (or investment dollars), for low-payback returns. You wouldn't invest your own money that way.

If the L&D system is supporting a Knowledge Management System, Human Capital or Competency effort, or populating their ERP systems, it should deliberately populate such a system for its "PUSH" audiences only.

A "PUSH" audience is one for which the Governance and Advisory System specifically targets and resources efforts to address an issue of sufficient magnitude. If the expenditures are to become investments with significant payback, the leaders of the Enterprise need to deliberately identify these PUSH targets and then resource the efforts for their required L&D development/ acquisition. And recognize that there will be life cycle costs for maintenance after the first costs are incurred.

Again, all L&D efforts for development and delivery should be for "PUSH" audiences only, and all content should be built specifically for them. L&D content is expensive in terms of both its initial costs and its life-cycle costs.

Design and development can be done in such a way that content chunks, also known as learning objects (as well as other names), are made deliberately for the PUSH audiences – but can also be made available as well to many "PULL" audiences, at a minimal incremental cost.

Never should the typically constrained resources of an Enterprise be invested in the "low-hanging fruit" of meeting the lower-payback needs of "PULL" audiences. PULL Target Audiences are by definition, not worth those direct investments.

The L&D staff assigned to this process collaborates with various Advisory groups representing their functions and any of their "owned" Enterprise processes. Functions, such as sales or finance, own certain systems and processes that include players from multiple functions. Think: cross-functional processes. This makes all of this a bit tricky; who funds the development of those folks from other functions?

Examples of PUSH Target Audiences outside of the process owners' realm include engineers involved in sales-owned proposal and bid process, or sales reps and engineers involved in finance-owned expense reimbursement process.

The various L&D product and service lines are determined by addressing these constituencies by their own Advisory group structure – but as reflected in priorities of another Advisory group. That's what makes it tricky – and requiring close collaboration. And why a Board of Governors needs to be involved in the final decision making. One groups highest priorities may not even be on the radar screen of another.

Advisory groups might be structured as simply as marketing and sales, engineering, manufacturing, staff, and management. Look at your organization chart and look at your core Value Chains.

Then take similar disciplines (such as accountant, engineers, writers), and organize them into learning communities, and establish an Advisory committee – after approval by the Board of Governors.

The Advisory groups are facilitated in this process to make their case to the Board of Governors as to what L&D efforts should take place, and they provide the business cases and justifications for each of their requests.

The Board of Governors will allocate the limited resources at their disposal to maximize returns. The Board of Governors may have already provided input to the Advisory groups initially as to where to focus their requests.

This Governance and Advisory approach helps balance there parochial needs of each advisory group and to better meet the current issues of the Enterprise as well as to prepare the Enterprise for its future.

Current critical needs and critical strategic needs should always get all of the resources, very deliberately, as determined by the Governance and Advisory System. That Area of Performance discussed in chapter 2, and drives the work of this AoP covered in this chapter.

Are Your Product and Service Line Program Management Processes Broken? Clues and Cues

Your L&D Product and Service Line Program Management Processes may be broken if:

- Projects undertaken by the L&D system are not the most critical to the Enterprise.
- Return on investment and economic value add forecasts do not exist, or suggest a low-payback for the efforts.
- You've spent hundreds of thousands of dollars to develop/acquire generic content, e.g., time management and communications skills, when strategic and/or critical Enterprise initiatives have been under-resourced in the past.

- No project management portfolio exists for the critical Target Audiences.
- The Portfolios are not aligned with the business' or the L&D organization's strategies.
- The Portfolio is not logical, and it doesn't align with functions and/or management's model of business; it's not an engineered architecture – it's a list of courses.

Processes Summary

The Product and Service Line Program Management Processes ensure that all product development efforts are targeted for significant payback areas.

Systematic efforts are made, involving all members of the Governance and Advisory Processes, to better ensure sufficient return on investment and economic value add for all projects and programs, and that those metrics are the drivers for making the tough allocation decisions.

Next, we'll look at the processes to design the Product and Service Line, the CAD – Curriculum Architecture design efforts.

L&D Product Line Design Processes

Processes Purpose

The Product Line Design Processes are a macro-ISD set of processes. My version of this is the **Curriculum Architecture Design - CAD** process. It is a systematic process for conducting the project planning, performance and enabling Knowledge/Skills analysis, the assessment of existing content for reuse potential and then the macro-design of L&D Paths, and finally the prioritization of any product line gaps and maintenance needs. The output of this is what a good Portfolio Management Plan contains.

A CAD effort is very different from the traditional ISD processes that develop only a or a small set of courses (or e-learning modules) as a "one-off" effort. Most ADDIE-like instructional development efforts are one-offs – and not governed by an overall architecture. That leads to inadvertent and costly content gaps and overlaps. And those gaps multiple in cost over their life cycle.

Processes Description

The Product Line Design Processes should look at the total needs of the critical PUSH Target Audience(s) to architect the product line and reuse content chunks where appropriate, to save large sums of money, time, and effort for both initial development costs and life-cycle costs for administration and maintenance.

The Product Line Design Processes design an entire product line of L&D products – and services as appropriate.

It does this incrementally by Target Audience(s), one at a time (or several in parallel), by systematically analyzing the critical performers' Performance Competence requirements within critical business processes, systematically determining the enabling knowledge and skill requirements, assessing the existing content for its reuse potential, and then designing the entire set of needs as an architecture – producing a performance-based Learning Path, T&D Path, L&D Path, etc.

Are Your Product Line Design Processes Broken? Clues and Cues

Your Product Line Design Processes may be broken if:

- Too many of your L&D efforts are "one-offs" and not part of a comprehensive effort to understand the total, critical needs of targeted audiences and address those high-payback needs on a priority basis.
- "Chunks"/products don't maximize potential for appropriate reuse.
- There are gaps in critical content.
- There is redundant content between products.
- L&D products don't directly target performance and impact performance adequately.
- Key, critical jobs do not have a logical menu and path for career development—members of key Target Audiences don't know what L&D to complete in what order.
- Your product offerings don't align with critical, high-payback business/ L&D strategies and needs.

Processes Summary

The Product Line Design Processes architect or engineer the product line using a reusable content chunk (object) strategy in a systematic manner. Priority gaps, in that architecture, are then targeted to be addressed in the system and processes that we'll cover in the next chapter.

The Product Line Design Processes create an architecture of modularized content subassemblies and products where shareable and unique modules of content are used to create performance-based products via courses; workshops; structured, on-the-job training; E-Learning programs; book reading assignments; project assignments; etc.

The intent is to define and design the entire architecture of all of the content products that *could be*, so that critical, high-payback business strategies and needs drive the prioritization of the content that *should be*, and the organization can be resourced appropriately to manage the system's processes and develop or acquire the content that *will be*.

Next, we'll look at the process to design the L&D Service Line.

Service Line Design Processes

Processes Purpose

The Service Line Design Processes is similar to the previous process, except that it macro-designs the *non-product* service line.

Those services might include performance improvement consultation, executive and manager coaching, job redesign, etc., depending on the capabilities of the system's personnel skills and the intentions of the Governance and Advisory System.

A non-product service is not a "widget," such as a course, book, video, seminar, etc. It could be something such as a "coaching service" that is provided to new supervisors. Or it could include a "Performance Improvement" consulting service – if that's what the Customers and Stakeholder require.

Processes Description

The Service Line Design Processes approach the need for other-than-product needs best met by the L&D resources versus other functions/organizations (TQM, industrial engineering, HR, etc.).

The best time to do this is within a CAD-like effort, covered previously. However there may be times when this needs to be done separately – or after a CAD has already been done.

For example, "executive coaching" or "facilitated mentoring" are services and not products. Conducting a Process Audit for your client is also a service and not a product. There are numerous services that an L&D organization might be expected to offer.

All of the potential non-product service offerings are determined and approved by the Governance and Advisory System before being built or bought via the next set of processes that we will cover.

Are Your Service Line Design Processes Broken? Clues and Cues

Your Service Line Design Processes may be broken if:

- Portions of the Enterprise are complaining of a lack of needed services from L&D or are recommending/demanding them.
- L&D service efforts are "one-offs" and not part of a comprehensive effort to understand the total, critical needs of targeted audiences, and then address and meet those high-payback needs with services on a priority basis. Perhaps you could offer coaching – but cannot afford to do that too!
- L&D services don't directly target high pay-back performance improvements.
- Service offerings don't align with critical, high-payback business/ L&D strategies and needs.

Processes Summary

This Service Line Design Processes determine the needs for high-payback, non-product services from the L&D system.

AoP Summary

This Area of Performance is about the Systems and its three Processes that deliberately analyze the needs of the key Target Audiences Enterprise for L&D products and services in a priority-driven manner, and then macro-design the solution set of products and/or services to meet the needs of the Enterprise.

There are simply too many needs, some with high-payback promise and many with low-, zero-, or negative-payback promise. The goal is to address the most critical needs first, and to *never* address many of the other, lower priority, lower payback needs.

Besides products, there could be service offerings from the L&D system, such as performance improvement consultation, executive and manager coaching, mentoring, job redesign, etc.

The many processes of the Product and Service Line Design System define and control the large-scale, business-critical programs (multi-project), as well as the small-scale, individual projects/products to develop or acquire. These are the products and services that are "by design" intended to be offered and rendered in the internal Enterprise marketplace to key customer groups.

Every Target Audience will not necessarily get the focused treatment of these processes – at least not if Return on Investment and Economic Value Add – or other key business metrics – are part of the allocation and business decision processes.

Only the needs of "PUSH" audiences should be resourced, and then are built to also meet some of the needs of "PULL" audiences with low incremental cost.

The Product and Service Line Design System's processes also define the high-priority, critical services that must be developed or acquired to support key customer strategies and tactics. Not every service provided to the Enterprise by the L&D organization has to be strictly training for the current job oriented. The decisions however, need to be conscious, business-oriented decisions, agreed to and approved by the L&D board of governors.

The formal Systems and Processes for addressing the Curriculum Manager's responsibilities include:

- Product and Service Line Program Management Processes
- Product Line Design Processes
- Service Line Design Processes

Part of your responsibility as a Curriculum Manager is to adopt and/ or adapt what has been presented here for your own context. Hopefully this has provided you with some guidance for doing that.

How Are You Currently Performing This Area of Performance Competence?

Regarding the Product & Service Line Design Area of Performance…

How are you currently **Planning this Work** – and how are you deciding what needs to get done, and by whom, and when?

What, if anything, needs to change?

How are you currently **Assigning this Work** – and how are you communicating the expectations of the work assignment?

What, if anything, needs to change?

How are you currently **Monitoring this Work** – and how are you focusing on the follow up monitoring of work processes and work products to insure that everything is okay?

What, if anything, needs to change?

How are you currently **Troubleshooting this Work** – and how are you following up for any of the work products or work processes where you spotted discrepancies, in order to resolve them?

What, if anything, needs to change?

Chapter Summary & Transition

This chapter was intended to address the processes of the L&D Product and Service Line Design System that are needed to define and architect or engineer the product and service lines in a very deliberate, systematic manner to ensure that the various Stakeholders of the Enterprise are served as optimally across the entire Enterprise (or major business units) as the key leaders deem appropriate.

Next, we'll review the Product and Service Line Development/ Acquisition System – where the ADDIE-like efforts are conducted to build or buy content per the architecture.

This chapter logically leads to the next, but your needs may cause you to want to skip around.

The list of chapters and their pages numbers are presented next for your personal navigation needs and desires.

1	What Does a Curriculum Manager Do?	1
2	AoP: Stakeholder Needs Assessment & Alignment	27
3	AoP: Strategic Planning & Management	53
4	AoP: Operations Planning & Management	65
5	AoP: Results Measurement	79
6	AoP: Improvement Planning	95
7	AoP: Communications	107
8	AoP: Product & Service Line Design	120
9	AoP: Product & Service Line Development	143
10	AoP: Product & Service Line Deployment	169
11	AoP: Process Design & Redesign	193
12	AoP: Human Assets	203
13	AoP: Environmental Assets	222
14	AoP: Special Assignments	241

| 15 | Summary & Close | 247 |
| 16 | Additional Related Resources & References | 254 |

Suggested Chapter Reflection & Reaction

I would suggest that prior to jumping into whichever chapter meets your needs that you give pause for a moment to reflect on the following and make some notes:

- What are your own "ah-ha's" so far?

- Are the Program Management and Macro-Design (Curriculum Architecture Design) Processes you have in place adequate to your needs? If not, what is the cost of the problem or opportunity, and what are the potential Returns for any Investments for improving these?

- How would you need to think about this model differently than it is presented?

- What language changes and deletions or additions might you need to make?

- What are all of the implications for you and your L&D function thus far?

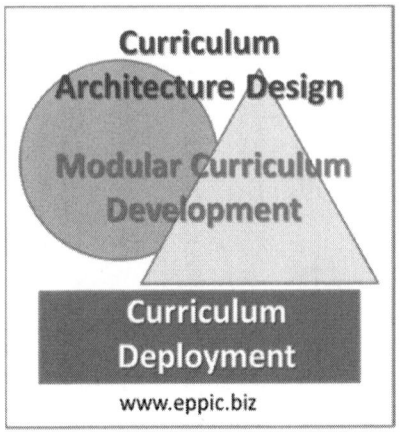

At the Core of a Curriculum Manager's
Performance Competence Requirements
are the architecture, development and deployment of
performance-enabling
Instructional and Informational Content

9 - AREA OF PERFORMANCE: PRODUCT & SERVICE LINE DEVELOPMENT

Chapter Overview

Read or scan this chapter if you are concerned with:

- **Product & Service Line Development** – the development and/or acquisition (make and/or buy) of the content called out in the prior Area of Performance: Product & Service Line Design – or for important "one-offs" as needed by your Customers and Stakeholders.

This chapter is intended to provide you with some details related to this Area of Performance and the formal Systems and Processes that you might adopt or adapt to meet your needs as a Curriculum Manager.

This is where ADDIE fits into the mix. My version of ADDIE, is the performance-based MCD – Modular Curriculum Development process of my PACT Processes for T&D, Learning and Knowledge Management. More on that later.

This chapter fits within the overall flow of the model as presented in the following graphic.

Curriculum Manager's Areas of Performance Competence Model

LEADERSHIP AoPs - Planning & Management
- ❏ Stakeholder Needs Assessment & Alignment
- ❏ Strategic Planning
- ❏ Operations Planning
- ❏ Results Measurement
- ❏ Improvement Planning
- ❏ Communications

CORE AoPs - Planning & Management
- ❏ Product & Service Line Design
- ❏ Product & Service Line Development
- ❏ Product & Service Line Deployment

SUPPORT AoPs - Planning & Management
- ❏ Process Design and Redesign
- ❏ Human Assets
- ❏ Environmental Assets
- ❏ Special Assignments

Adapted from the Management Areas of Performance Model
©2002 Guy W. Wallace

As you read through this chapter keep in mind your potential need to adapt this content to your context – or to adapt your context to this content.

AoP: C2- Product & Service Line Development

AoP Overview

Properly designed, modular, performance-based L&D content and services, will meet current needs better and will improve ROI; and is more robust to future changes and will also minimize the total life-cycle costs – further improving life cycle ROI.

If they are cost-conscious at all, too many L&D organizations still focus on minimizing initial development costs: first costs. They typically don't understand the life-cycle costs. And while improving the short term ROI with that short term focus, they can inadvertently ruin the long term ROI – and even take it negative!

They would serve the shareholders/owners better if they were focused on reducing overall life-cycle costs and improving overall life cycle ROI.

Life-cycle costs include first costs for development and implementation, but they also include administration costs, storage costs, maintenance costs and other operating costs for other L&D systems and processes – for each L&D product or service. There is tremendous pressure in the L&D world to reduce costs or increase cost-efficiency – but it shouldn't always be limited to first costs! That is Penny-wise and Pound foolish – as that old saying goes – which is to say in the USA: Dime-wise and Dollar-foolish.

Increasing the value of L&D interventions requires investments in improvement of the L&D organization's processes, people and infrastructure systems and other environmental support systems. Total Investment Costs (all costs) need to be compared to the potential Total Returns (all Returns) – to determine the Total Return on Investment potential. And yes, not every Return can be converted to dollars. Sometimes just avoiding or minimizing the chance of catastrophic Risks is a good enough reason; a reasonable Return on Investment. No calculations required. One of the no-brainers, if you will.

Once that has been determined, the ROI potential, then informed business decisions can be made.

The opportunity to spend the Enterprise's limited capital resources, entrusted to L&D's Curriculum Managers in terms of improvements to the processes, people, facilities, equipment, materials, and budgets, etc., provided by the organization, always needs to be compared to the return on investment opportunities everywhere else in the Enterprise.

Perhaps those funds should go to the Sales function instead. Or perhaps they should go to L&D to make improvements in how they do business in producing the needed L&D products and services.

This issue is not unique to L&D products and services. Many companies have addressed problems and/or opportunities by reducing their internal costs by using common processes, systems, and tools/techniques – or developing the people in those processes better than the current state is currently doing.

The auto industry faced this need back in the late 1970s and '80s and then changed their production and operations methods based on a theory of common-ization of both their processes and systems. This became known as Lean Manufacturing decades ago – but is not unique to Manufacturing. This is also not very different from standardizing the "flint lock" system for rifles over two hundred years ago.

Use of Knowledge Management Systems (KMS) can also be used to leverage performance capability better in the moment of need, and to facilitate organizational development prior to the moment of need via coaching or mentoring or Informal Learning means – where the Learner is "on their own."

The trick for KMS is to tie the content to specific Processes – and not just dump it all into this electronic repository and enable "search" functionality. Getting 3,000 or 300 or 30 hits for a search is really not all that helpful.

AoP Typical Outputs

- Training content of many blends in terms of media and modes

- Learning content of many blends in terms of media and modes

- Knowledge Management content of many blends in terms of media and modes

Today there is much confusion with these labels within the L&D world. So if it makes sense to you and your context – blend them all into "one phrase" or two, such as L&D or T&D, as I have been doing since the beginning of this book – or displace that phrase and these three labels – with whatever is appropriate to your context. A rose is a rose is a rose – most of the time.

AoP Typical Tasks

Even though it generates much controversy – the tasks are based on the ADDIE model, with a slight change:

- **Project Planning & Kick-Off** – planning of the tasks and personnel required for the project and ensuring the support of key customers and Stakeholders via a kick-off meeting to finalize the plan and schedule.

- **Analysis** – of the Target Audience, the performance competence requirements, the enabling knowledge and skills required and the existing content and its potential reuse, as is or after modification.

- **Design** – of the content's information, demonstrations and application exercises to enable performance competence.

- **Development** – of the content per the design, plus alpha and beta testing as needed.

- **Pilot-Test** – of the entire product with typical Target Audience members.

- **Revision & Release** – post-Pilot-Test revisions and then release to the Master materials system, and ongoing Deployment and Access systems.

There is a great deal of controversy about ADDIE currently – in fact it's been a controversy that recycles itself every few years – as I believe that this is the 5th or 6th time I've seen it in the past 30 years.

Personally I believe that the controversy about "ADDIE" is from those who have not figured out how to flex this model – and see every suggested task as needed – as they haven't really designed their downstream processes tight enough to understand what they need from upstream, and what they don't need.

And many don't see it as a Project Planning framework – and they expect its use to design instructional content well.

It won't. That's the difference between Processes – and Practices. You need both.

And too often they don't start with authentic Performance Competence Requirements as their terminal learning **and** performance goals – which define how to measure the success of any L&D intervention.

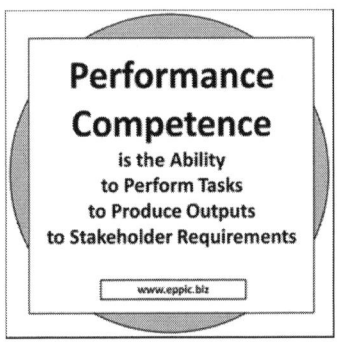

By now you should be acutely aware of my focus on Stakeholders and Processes Performance.

Here is a model of my version of ADDIE – which I label/market as Modular Curriculum Development (MCD):

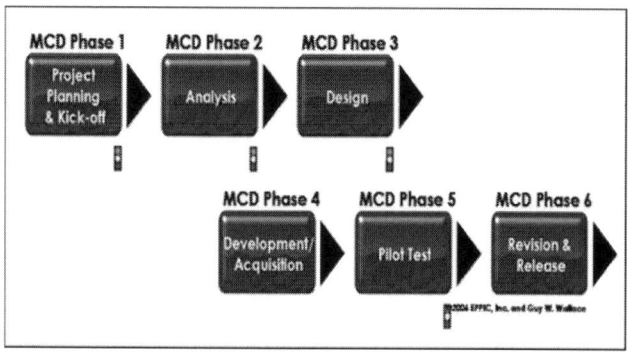

I have been using this approach – and an earlier version of this - to structure my ISD efforts since 1979 – with **Planning always coming before Analysis**. Always!

Evaluation, both formative and summative happen throughout - at every phase – via my use of a Group Process with project Clients, Master Performers and other Subject Matter Experts.

This MCD model and the details underneath it do not design your content – they simply guide your process – your tasks to produce outputs to Stakeholder requirements – when you employ sound/valid instructional design practices and principles in this predictable.

My ADDIE-like approach – helps plan and manage projects – from a time and budget perspective – as it is a project management scheme. My ISD Practices are framed by this ISD Process. Your adapted version should as well.

As we will see – there is more to this AoP than new product development – or existing product maintenance.

AoP Systems & Processes Overview

Next we will look at a formal System for addressing this AoP:

- **Product & Service Development**

This system's processes organize the efforts to build, buy and use, or buy and modify, and then maintain L&D content consistent with the performance-based requirements and the product & service line architecture designs, from a Curriculum Architecture Design effort – or for priority one-offs.

These expensive efforts – as developing training is always expensive – are always done in order to meet only the high-payback, critical business needs of the Enterprise, not every need uncovered.

L&D efforts should be avoided, or approached with the lowest cost solution. It needs to be both effective and efficient in meeting those Performance Competence requirements of the Target Audiences that have been deemed worthy by the Governance and Advisory System.

Always! As good stewardship of shareholder equity demands!

The following five Processes of this System will be reviewed next:

- Product and Service Line Development and Acquisition Program Management Processes
- Modular Curriculum Development Processes
- Purchased Product Acquisition Processes

- Purchased Product Modification Processes
- Existing Content Maintenance Processes

Let's now look at the first of these.

Product and Service Line Development and Acquisition Program Management Processes

Processes Purpose

The Product and Service Line Development and Acquisition Program Management Processes are intended to deliberately control the multiple efforts for development and/or acquisition for putting the high-priority, high-payback products and services in place.

This is Program Management – or Portfolio Management – versus simple Project Management of your development efforts.

Processes Description

The Product and Service Line Development and Acquisition Program Management Processes provide the program-level Command and Control (and targeted empowerment) that is very necessary in this Internet-speed world in which we live.

Command and Control by the Customers and Stakeholders does not necessarily need to proceed and operate in slow motion if your processes are well specified, defined, and developed. On the other hand you need to be careful about going too fast.

Too much is at stake in the high priority targeted investments – and "haste makes waste."

The need to avoid waste, of course, has to be balanced with the need for rapid responses to meet fast-moving issues and needs. But most of the needs to go fast are due to needing to be reactive because you and your systems/processes aren't proactive – enough.

We probably do not subscribe to the notion that "whatever, whenever, however" as being okay when it comes to our house purchase, our life savings and retirement investment strategies, where our kids go to school and college, and what kind of training and car we put our new 16-year-old drivers in.

And so it goes for the not-so-minor investments in human competence development needed to deal with current issues and/or move the Enterprise forward into its future. Approaching these in a "whatever, whenever, however" mode is probably a very bad idea.

Assuming that the number of L&D products and services that you need to either develop, acquire, modify, or maintain is large, careful control will be necessary to safeguard both the shareholders' and other Stakeholders' interests.

Again, L&D is very expensive. Initial costs can be very high. Life-cycle costs are too often an afterthought in many situations and are also very expensive, more expensive.

You not only need to ask "if we are willing to build it, will they come?" but also "if we are willing to build it, are we willing to maintain it?" And then ask, "What does that do to Return on Investment – and the economic value add (EVA)?"

What are the life cycle perspectives of the ROI and EVA?

The same is true for services as well as products. Why build it if you're not willing to project future needed life-cycle costs for maintenance and administration? Too often L&D is built or acquired without the due diligence of simply asking and determining "what else have we purposely or inadvertently signed ourselves up for" in terms of the costs over the long haul.

And that is simply poor stewardship.

Are Your Product and Service Line Development and Acquisition Program Management Processes Broken? Clues and Cues

Your Product and Service Line Development and Acquisition Program Management Processes may be broken if:

- You can't measure positive return on investment and economic value add actuals against plans for products/services.
- Product and service development is being done because someone internal to the L&D system thinks it's a good idea—the portfolio is not being managed.
- Products and services developed aren't maintained due to resource constraints.
- Resources are not reallocated as needed based on changes in business direction.
- You don't know what to work on next if a project is completed early.
- Projects are not sequenced to take appropriate advantage of synergies (e.g., similar content/subject matter experts between projects).

Processes Summary

The Product and Service Line Development and Acquisition Program Management Processes are intended to deliberately control the development and acquisition processes needed to put high-priority, high-payback products and services into place as determined in the prior AoP that we covered in the last chapter.

It's either that or "whatever, whenever, however."

And that's no way to run an Enterprise's L&D organization. Even if the Enterprise were in a position for self-actualizing, and can afford anything and everything – that is a temporary situation at best in today's world.

> **I believe: that it's still a business decision, even for a learning organization.**

I hope you do as well.

Next, we'll review the Modular Curriculum Development process, where traditional ISD happens. This could be for one of the many projects within the Development/ Acquisition Program Management portfolio that we just covered – or for some important "one-offs!"

Modular Curriculum Development Processes

Processes Purpose

The Modular Curriculum Development Processes are a formal ISD process to develop performance-based content, or minimally, performance-relevant awareness, knowledge, and skills developing content. This process can be done via insourcing, outsourcing, or a combination of the two.

Anything other than a formal process to develop performance-based content is equivalent to figuratively taking Enterprise dollars and burning them in the headquarters' parking lot.

That is actually cheaper than building ill-advised content development or purchase (other than it being against the law to do so, in some places).

If you burn the money (figuratively) of first costs, you can avoid the wasted money of the life cycle costs.

It's those other costs for deployment and other life-cycle costs that we could then avoid, which only add to the shareholder loss.

Processes Description

The Modular Curriculum Development Processes build custom training & development, as opposed to purchasing content products for deployment.

The content could take the form of group-paced; self-paced; or structured on-the-job training.

The ISD process generally known as ADDIE is used to build content. ADDIE is akin to almost any "new product development process" model used today in many Enterprises and in many development-oriented functions. All engineering functions have an equivalent.

Are Your Modular Curriculum Development Processes Broken? Clues and Cues

Your Modular Curriculum Development Processes could be broken if:

- Your content does not meet the established objectives for transferring awareness, knowledge, or skills to the Target Audiences' jobs.
- Your content development efforts are somewhat ad hoc, not in control, and not predictable in terms of their eventual costs or cycle times.
- Your content development does not design and build appropriately reusable "chunks" of content for sharing with other Target Audiences.

Processes Summary

The Modular Curriculum Development Processes develop L&D product offerings.

These could be group-paced; self-paced; and structured, on-the-job training. The offerings should be performance-based or, minimally, performance relevant. Content products can deploy and create awareness, knowledge, and skills in their Target Audiences.

Next, we'll review the Purchased Product Acquisition Processes, where content is bought, not built.

Purchased Product Acquisition Processes

Processes Purpose

The Purchased Product Acquisition Processes are formal processes in place to buy L&D for use as is or for modification prior to use or deployment.

Processes Description

The Purchased Product Acquisition Processes are similar to the last processes, where content is built - content products.

This process also uses the ADDIE model, but only as a starting point. The major difference in the Purchased Product Acquisition Processes are that in ADDIE's step three, development, the content is bought instead of built.

Buying is often cheaper, but may get you generic content, missing the "how to apply this in my job setting" spin that is necessary for "transfer back to the job" to have a chance at actually occurring. Authenticity counts!

Research has shown how important content authenticity is to actual learning – and making sure that your content is authentic enough is key. Doing the upfront analysis and then pilot-testing are critical steps that are too often are just not done. Saving time and money – or so those decision makers think.

But the Design step is also important in that it lets you know what you might be looking for during your "shopping" efforts.

Therefore, to make decisions rapidly and correctly, your ADDIE-type process needs to be designed to accommodate both a buy and build (if you cannot find what you need) development approach.

The next process in this chapter is where any modifications that need to be made to the purchased content happen. If the Target Audiences' needs specifications cannot be met exactly with the purchased product, then modifications may be needed, if legally doable.

Sometimes all you can do is buy a product and augment it with other content versus modify it. It all depends on what you bought and the terms and conditions of that sale. Do the "legal thing," please.

Are Your Purchased Product Acquisition Processes Broken? Clues and Cues

Your Purchased Product Acquisition Processes may be broken if:

- L&D bought often doesn't make the grade in terms of creating the awareness, knowledge, and skills as measured in the Target Audiences during/after the L&D deployment.
- It takes too long to evaluate and decide on which L&D you should purchase.

Processes Summary

The Purchased Product Acquisition Processes are a rational business processes needed to safeguard the shareholders and other Enterprise Stakeholders. It needs to reflect the principles and practices of good ISD.

Next, let's review the process to modify purchased L&D, as necessary to the situation.

L&D Purchased Product Modification Processes

Processes Purpose

The Purchased Product Modification Processes are formal processes used to make modifications or augmentations to purchased products, depending on the legalities of making modifications to potentially copyrighted content, per the terms and conditions of your purchase.

And you may need to make modification to content developed (built) internally, that you own, for other Target Audiences when that content isn't authentic enough for the additional audiences.

Active Listening for one audience may be very different than for the next audience.

Processes Description

The Purchased Product Modification Processes need to practice good ISD. This is where any content bought – or is otherwise available – isn't a good enough fit and needs to be modified to better meet the specific needs of the intended Target Audience(s) for authenticity.

This is also where custom information, demonstrations and application exercises, might be built to augment and support the purchased product.

In the "modular/object oriented/chunked" world of both e-learning (electronic) and some traditional learning design philosophies, modifying or augmenting existing L&D may or may not be a big deal.

Here it depends on the terms and conditions of the sale for any purchased products. If you built it – you own it – and can augment it in any manner. That's covered next.

After the rework (adds, deletes, and modifications), a full pilot test is conducted, and then post-pilot revisions are made as needed.

Are Your Purchased Product Modification Processes Broken? Clues and Cues

Your Purchased Product Modification Processes may be broken if:

- You have/have had any legal issues (lawsuits, complaints, or future risks) resulting from making modifications to copyrighted materials.
- The cycle times and costs for making modifications are not reliably predictable.
- Content bought and modified often doesn't make the grade in terms of creating the awareness, knowledge, and skills as measured in their Target Audiences during/after the deployment.

Processes Summary

The Purchased Product Modification Processes are ISD processes that takes the content that is bought or otherwise available, as well as the front-end data from the planning and analysis efforts, and completes the ISD process by reworking the "bought/available" materials – always within the legal restrictions of any copyright laws and any purchase agreements with the copyright owners.

Next, we'll look at the process to maintain existing content.

Existing Content Maintenance Processes

Processes Purpose

The Existing Content Maintenance Processes allow any existing product to be updated as needed. It employs sound ISD processes. It uses the original project analysis data, as available, and may revalidate that before moving forward with updates.

Processes Description

The Existing Content Maintenance Processes are equivalent to the product development processes. One might move more quickly through its phases and tasks, because it may simply need to validate the analysis data rather than create that data.

Are Your Existing Content Maintenance Processes Broken? Clues and Cues

Your Existing Content Maintenance Processes may be broken if:

- Products are still being deployed or accessed that are in need of updating.
- Updating cycle times and costs cannot be reasonably predicted.
- You never stop updating.
- Maintenance is not a planned, resourced or prioritized project effort.

Processes Summary

The Existing Content Maintenance Processes need to practice good ISD. It needs to be a process in control. It needs to be directed by the Governance and Advisory System to meet the highest priority needs of the Enterprise.

Note: An alternative to maintenance is always deletion from the product line.

If the costs of keeping, deploying, or maintaining certain content are greater than its returns to the Enterprise, it is a drain on shareholder equity and should be dropped. It is a "money loser" even if there is a real audience for the product.

It is still a business decision, even for a learning organization.

AoP Summary

This Area of Performance is about Maintenance of Content.

The formal Systems and Processes for addressing the Curriculum Manager's responsibilities include:

- Product and Service Line Development and Acquisition Program Management Processes
- Modular Curriculum Development Processes
- Purchased Product Acquisition Processes
- Purchased Product Modification Processes
- Existing Content Maintenance Processes

Part of your responsibility as a Curriculum Manager is to adopt and/ or adapt what has been presented here for your own context. Hopefully this has provided you with some guidance for doing that.

How Are You Currently Performing This Area of Performance Competence?

Regarding the Product & Service Line Development Area of Performance…

How are you currently **Planning this Work** – and how are you deciding what needs to get done, and by whom, and when?

What, if anything, needs to change?

How are you currently **Assigning this Work** – and how are you communicating the expectations of the work assignment?

What, if anything, needs to change?

How are you currently **Monitoring this Work** – and how are you focusing on the follow up monitoring of work processes and work products to insure that everything is okay?

What, if anything, needs to change?

How are you currently **Troubleshooting this Work** – and how are you following up for any work products or work process where you spotted discrepancies, in order to resolve them?

What, if anything, needs to change?

Chapter Summary & Transition

This chapter was intended to address the five processes of the L&D Product and Service Line Development/Acquisition System to develop and acquire content products consistent with the directives of the Governance and Advisory System.

These processes ensure that the product and service offerings are appropriate to the high-priority, high-payback problems and opportunities of the Enterprise, as seen by the Governance and Advisory System Customers and Stakeholders.

Next, we'll view the Product and Service Line Deployment System.

This chapter logically leads to the next, but your needs may cause you to want to skip around.

The list of chapters and their pages numbers are presented next for your personal navigation needs and desires.

1	What Does a Curriculum Manager Do?	1
2	AoP: Stakeholder Needs Assessment & Alignment	27
3	AoP: Strategic Planning & Management	53
4	AoP: Operations Planning & Management	65
5	AoP: Results Measurement	79
6	AoP: Improvement Planning	95

7	AoP: Communications	107
8	AoP: Product & Service Line Design	120
9	AoP: Product & Service Line Development	143
10	AoP: Product & Service Line Deployment	169
11	AoP: Process Design & Redesign	193
12	AoP: Human Assets	203
13	AoP: Environmental Assets	222
14	AoP: Special Assignments	241
15	Summary & Close	247
16	Additional Related Resources & References	254

Suggested Chapter Reflection & Reaction

I would suggest that prior to jumping into whichever chapter meets your needs that you give pause for a moment to reflect on the following and make some notes:

- What are your own "ah-ha's" so far?

- Are the Design (including analysis and development) Processes you have in place adequate to your needs? If not, what is the cost of the problem or opportunity, and what are the potential Returns for any Investments for improving these?

- How would you need to think about this model differently than it is presented?

- What language changes and deletions or additions might you need to make?

- What are all of the implications for you and your L&D function thus far?

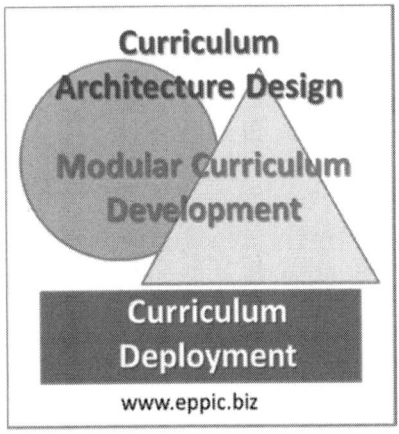

At the Core of a Curriculum Manager's
Performance Competence Requirements
are the architecture, development and deployment of
performance-enabling
Instructional and Informational Content

10 - AREA OF PERFORMANCE: PRODUCT & SERVICE LINE DEPLOYMENT

Chapter Overview

Read or scan this chapter if you are concerned with:

- **Product & Service Line Deployment** – which organizes the operations of the L&D distribution and access channels.

This chapter is intended to provide you with some details related to this Area of Performance

C3- Product & Service Line Deployment – is where you deliver or make accessible your L&D products and services.

As you read through this chapter keep in mind your potential need to adapt this content to your context – or to adapt your context to this content.

This chapter fits within the overall flow of the model as presented in the following graphic.

Curriculum Manager's Areas of Performance Competence Model

LEADERSHIP AoPs - Planning & Management
- ❏ Stakeholder Needs Assessment & Alignment
- ❏ Strategic Planning
- ❏ Operations Planning
- ❏ Results Measurement
- ❏ Improvement Planning
- ❏ Communications

CORE AoPs - Planning & Management
- ❏ Product & Service Line Design
- ❏ Product & Service Line Development
- ❏ Product & Service Line Deployment

SUPPORT AoPs - Planning & Management
- ❏ Process Design and Redesign
- ❏ Human Assets
- ❏ Environmental Assets
- ❏ Special Assignments

Adapted from the Management Areas of Performance Model
©2002 Guy W. Wallace

AoP: C3- Product & Service Line Deployment

AoP Overview

This system's processes deliver via people and non-people-based mechanisms, or a combination of the two in a blend, performance-based content – for use in the moment of need and/or prior to the moment of need. They also enable planning and ordering for some of the Products and Services offered, as needed.

All of the methods and media that are feasible within the Enterprise and for the specific Target Audiences need to be considered when making the packaging decisions in the prior systems Design and Development AoPs covered in the prior two chapters.

In this system the packaged content is stored, maintained, and used for delivery and/or access.

Audiences, customers, shareholders, and Stakeholders shape the way L&D is deployed and accessed. One method and one size do not fit all situational needs.

AoP Typical Outputs

- Master Materials Storage Systems
- Master Materials Change Management Processes
- Scheduling Processes
- Facilitator and Coach Development and Certification Processes
- Facilitator-led Content Deployment Processes
- Self-paced Content Deployment Processes

- Coached/Mentored Content Deployment Processes
- Individual Development Planning Processes
- Ordering and Registration Processes

AoP Typical Tasks

- Creating and managing a Master Materials Storage capability and Retrieval Processes
- Creating a Master Materials Change Management Processes
- Creating and managing a Scheduling Processes
- Creating and managing a Facilitator and Coach Development and Certification Processes
- Creating and managing a Facilitator-led Content Deployment Processes
- Creating and managing a Self-paced Content Deployment Processes
- Creating and managing a Coached/Mentored Content Deployment Processes
- Creating and managing an Individual Development Planning Processes
- Creating and managing an Ordering and Registration Processes

AoP Systems & Processes Overview

Next we will look at a formal System for addressing this Area of Performance:

- **Product & Service Line Deployment**

The following nine Processes of this System will be reviewed next:

- Master Materials Storage and Retrieval Processes
- Master Materials Change Management Processes
- Scheduling Processes
- Facilitator and Coach Development and Certification Processes
- Facilitator-led Content Deployment Processes
- Self-paced Content Deployment Processes
- Coached/Mentored Content Deployment Processes
- Individual Development Planning Processes
- Ordering and Registration Processes

Let's start.

L&D Master Materials Storage and Retrieval Processes

Processes Purpose

The Master Materials Storage and Retrieval Processes stores all material masters for access by developers and delivery staff.

Processes Description

Deployment staff will need the masters to deploy the Product Content or Services, whether paper masters or electronic masters.

Development staff may need to update content, and delivery and/or administrative staff will pull those master materials (depending on the deployment channel used for delivery that impacts content packaging) to reproduce learner materials and instructor, facilitator, coach or mentor materials used in the delivery.

Development staff may also need to pull materials for reuse purposes with other Target Audiences and for reuse in other Delivery/Deployment Events. If the content is being deployed over the Internet or Enterprise intranet, the original masters (used for uploading into those systems) are still archived in this system.

Version control is a key issue. A question to ask is whether or not the materials could or should be used during the update process. Obviously, content that deals with laws, regulations, and codes that have changed should be taken out of use until updated.

The voice of the Governance and Advisory System needs to be heard, as well as any "content product line manager" who can best make the appropriate decision as to what risks exist for out-of-date content and what to do about it.

Are Your Master Materials Storage and Retrieval Processes Broken? Clues and Cues

Your Master Materials Storage and Retrieval Processes may be broken if:

- It is too difficult to retrieve material masters for updating or deployment purposes.
- It is too difficult to access current content to attempt reuse.
- Materials are used in deployment when the intent should have been to make them unavailable during updates.
- There is no version control of material masters that ensures all materials are up to date.

Processes Summary

The Master Materials Storage and Retrieval Processes archive/keep all of the current material masters needed to support ongoing deployment of the content for Products and for Services.

It handles all materials appropriate to the delivery/ deployment channels being used, and functions as the central storage repository of material masters to facilitate content updating/ maintenance needs.

Next, we'll view the Master Materials Change Management Processes, where the actual changes (updates) to the material masters are completed.

L&D Master Materials Change Management Processes

Processes Purpose

The Master Materials Change Management Processes are responsible for displacing the old content with the new and making sure that the old doesn't inadvertently get out along with the new content.

Processes Description

The Master Materials Change Management Processes take the updated materials from the Existing Content Maintenance Processes, and replaces/displaces the old with the new.

It's that simple, unless your situation is overly complicated and out of control because you don't have the other processes in place and in control.

Are Your Master Materials Change management Processes Broken? Clues and Cues

Your Master Materials Change Management Processes may be broken if:

- Outdated materials are still being used in deployment after updating.

Processes Summary

In summary, the Master Materials Change Management Processes of the L&D system captures the changes to the content (or any other change) and updates the master materials files (paper files and/or electronic files).

Next, we'll view the Scheduling Processes, where that type of content that needs to be scheduled – is scheduled for future deliveries/deployments.

L&D Scheduling Processes

Processes Purpose

The Scheduling Processes are used to develop market-demand schedules for delivery of any content type that is scheduled and not on-demand.

Processes Description

Not all content types are scheduled, nor should they be. Web/Internet deployments or accessible may or may not be scheduled. The types of Web/ Internet deployments that may need to be scheduled are synchronous type events with a limit put on their attendance.

The point is that the schedule demands of the marketplace should be the starting point for any process to dictate the schedule for making those types of content available. It should be based on the forecast demand, but it can also be used reactively after a specific delivery has been requested.

This process requires something at the front end that gathers information about the "when" do they want it. The answer for this is to have a development plan for participation for each and every employee targeted ("PUSH or PULL" audiences) in the Enterprise and for critical nonemployees as well if those are in your Target Audiences.

Of course, not everyone will participate and attend/complete product offerings per their original development plan, but models can be built over time to better adjust the demand forecast. This issue – of demand forecasts that are not being perfect forecasts – is nothing new as most businesses must try to guess the consumption of their products and services in order to avoid their own over-stock or under-stock situations.

Are Your Scheduling Processes Broken? Clues and Cues

Your Scheduling Processes may be broken if:

- There are complaints from the Target Audience about availability of your offerings.

- Seats (or site spaces) go underused or seats/spaces are backlogged.
- Materials are overstocked or under-stocked (unavailable) when requested.

Processes Summary

The Scheduling Processes schedule all Products and Services that requires scheduling. The customer voice-driven schedules are based on their forecasted demands based on their formal development plans – and amended as trends dictate.

Next, we'll look at the Processes for preparing the facilitators and coaches for those Products/ Services requiring those human delivery supports.

Facilitator and Coach Development and Certification Processes

Processes Purpose

The Facilitator and Coach Development and Certification Processes are used to prepare the humans needed for any deployment and/or deployment support.

Processes Description

The Facilitator and Coach Development and Certification Processes ensure the quality of the instructors/facilitators and the coaches/mentors required to deploy and support the Product/ Service deployment.

Not all Products need humans in these roles, but some do. Sometimes known as 3T or TTT or train-the-trainer, these processes are critical to every deployment method other than self-paced.

Where appropriate, and as typically specified in the original design and final deployment strategies and plans, instructors, facilitators, coaches, and other support staff/help desk individuals must be prepared for their jobs if this was deemed a necessary offering.

Sometimes a facilitator only needs to be trained. But sometimes the process needs to go beyond simply training them to a higher level of certifying them, due to either regulatory requirements or because it's the smart thing to do.

Sometimes support personnel, as with a help desk model, need to be prepared to assist the learners and others involved in the deployment process (facilitators, coaches, and administrators).

Are Your Facilitator and Coach Development and Certification Processes Broken? Clues and Cues

Your L&D Facilitator and Coach Development and Certification Processes may be broken if:

- There is an insufficient number of staff to deploy L&D per the demand.
- Evaluation feedback identifies any problems with the knowledge, skills, and attitudes/demeanor of the facilitators, coaches, or other support staff.

Processes Summary

The Facilitator and Coach Development and Certification Processes ensure the quality of the instructors/facilitators, coaches/mentors, and other support and administration staff (per the design) required to deploy the Product/Service.

Next, we'll view the Facilitator-led Deployment Processes.

Facilitator-led Deployment Processes

Processes Purpose

The Facilitator-led Deployment Processes control the deployment of all instructor-led/facilitator-led Products/Services.

Processes Description

The Facilitator-led Deployment Processes get this type of content out the door, per the schedule established in the previous process. It is ongoing delivery/deployment.

From initial scheduling of the specific instructors/facilitators, to arranging for the delivery site specifics (rooms, furniture, equipment, and materials), to the actual delivery, and through the final evaluations conducted, this process makes it all happen.

This effort can be quite complex in large organizations.

Are Your Facilitator-led Deployment Processes Broken? Clues and Cues

Your Facilitator-led Deployment Processes may be broken if:

- Feedback from delivery evaluations (learners, instructors, administrative, etc.) suggests problems from their perspectives, with things other than facilitator credibility or content accuracy, completeness, and appropriateness, but including non-content items such as the room, facility, and equipment issues.

Processes Summary

The Facilitator-led Deployment Processes are the ongoing delivery process for group-paced content.

Next, we'll examine the Self-paced Deployment Processes.

Self-paced L&D Deployment Processes

Processes Purpose

The Self-paced Deployment Processes handle the deployment of all learner-controlled (self-paced) content.

Processes Description

The Self-paced Deployment Processes sometimes responds to orders placed for this type of content, ships it out to the recipient, and then follows up with whatever is appropriate (reinforcement text messages, coaching sessions, evaluations, etc.) per the initial design and the final deployment and evaluation strategies.

It might be as simple as publishing "e" content to the Web, or to your Knowledge Management System (KMS), or to your learning management system (LMS).

Shipping products may be included, unless these are simply downloadable from the Enterprise intranet. Again, as always, it depends.

And this process may also facilitate the collection of any data such as evaluation data, and/or any home work done by the learners before or after the main Event – whatever its mode.

Are Your Self-Paced Deployment Processes Broken? Clues and Cues

Your Self-paced Deployment Processes may be broken if:

- Feedback from evaluations suggests problems from the learners' perspective for things other than content accuracy, completeness, and appropriateness, including items such as availability, timeliness of receipt, or accessibility.

Processes Summary

In summary, the Self-paced Deployment Processes of the Product & Service Line Deployment System ships content, either physically or virtually (electronically), and makes these Products/Services available or accessible.

Next, we'll view the Coached/Mentored Deployment Processes.

Coached/Mentored L&D Deployment Processes

Processes Purpose

The Coached/Mentored Deployment Processes deploy all Products/Services requiring the use of coaches and mentors to support the learners.

Processes Description

The Coached/Mentored Deployment Processes provide for the delivery of all coached and mentored Products/ Services, with the assistance of designated and perhaps certified coaches or mentors.

This type of content is very much like group-paced content; only the coach or mentor provides some one-on-one (or one-on-a-small-group) interaction on-the-job or in some other designated facility/space – instead of an instructor/facilitator dealing with many learners, most likely in a traditional classroom setting.

This type of Product/ Service is also very much like self-paced content because it offers more flexibility (depending on whom the learner is or who the coach is) in timing, focus, and pacing. The coach/mentor is given structured content materials to guide their delivery, allowing for local customization if needed.

The coaches and mentors can be certified as needed/warranted by the topic or as dictated by law or regulation.

Are Your Coached/ Mentored Deployment Processes Broken? Clues and Cues

Your Coached/Mentored Deployment Processes may be broken if:

- Feedback from delivery evaluations (learners, instructors, administrative, etc.) suggests problems from the learners' perspective with things other than coach/mentor credibility or content accuracy, completeness, and appropriateness, including non-content items such as room, facility, and equipment issues.

Processes Summary

The Coached/Mentored Deployment Processes delivers all L&D designed for delivery that is supported by coaches/mentors.

Next we'll look at the Individual Development Planning Processes.

Individual Development Planning Processes

Processes Purpose

The Individual Planning Processes are used for planning an individual employee's development, but also for compiling (rolling up), locally or Enterprise-wide, all of the plans in order to place a "demand forecast" on the deployment/delivery systems.

Processes Description

The Individual Development Planning Processes can be manual and on paper, or it can be accomplished using sophisticated electronic tools, which many learning management systems (LMS) today enable.

The goal is to allow learners and their management to deliberately plan on development participation that is consistent with the needs and constraints of the business, and whether they need to stay focused on the short term performance needs - or that they need to look further out into the future and get ready for that now.

They might need to start planning and implementing development plans to grow staff to meet future needs or to prepare for future job changes, such as promotions or lateral moves across the organization.

Individual needs vary within larger Enterprises, so a one-size approach or philosophy to participation won't necessarily meet the needs of the Enterprise very well.

The goal is to prioritize development participation to ensure human competence in the right amount and the right time in the right Enterprise processes for return on investment and economic value add at the Enterprise level.

Are Your Individual Development Planning Processes Broken? Clues and Cues

Your Individual Development Planning Processes may be broken if:

- There are no individual-to-group-to-Enterprise roll-ups of the participation plans. They are all discrete and not linked.

- Individual plans are not used and/or no common format exists.
- No one has a realistic clue of the future demand for development products and services.
- Seats and sites are under-filled or sites are underutilized for many deployments.
- Seats and sites demand outstrips availability.

Processes Summary

In summary, the Individual Development Planning Processes of the Product & Service Line Deployment systems provides a management planning, monitoring, and control tool at the local, unit, or Enterprise levels.

It also provides a "heads-up" to the deployment/delivery systems on who wants what Product/ Services when. This provides for better, more efficient scheduling of those Product/ Services that need to be scheduled.

Next, we'll view the Ordering and Registration Processes where the customer (the learner) and their management both *time* and *place* their bets as to the timing of their need and the potential returns versus the costs to them for participating.

L&D Ordering and Registration Processes

Processes Purpose

The Ordering and Registration Processes is where the customers can place their orders appropriate to the type of products/services offered.

Processes Description

The Ordering and Registration Processes are used for obtaining a seat in classroom deliveries or ordering books, videos, and audios, etc. It isn't used when e-learning or audio and video podcasts are individually taken and is available on demand via the Enterprise Web site or the Enterprise intranet. Or when audio or video programs (on CD or DVD discs or on older VHS tapes) are not allowed to be put on the web by the Enterprise due to copyright issues, etc.

At other places in the Enterprise, this process may be known as order fulfillment. Customers place orders and then their orders are fulfilled.

Are Your Ordering and Registration Processes Broken? Clues and Cues

Your Ordering and Registration Processes may be broken if:

- Customers complain that their "orders" are not being filled in a timely manner or are being filled incorrectly.
- Expediting orders is usually necessary and taking a lot of people's time and attention.

Processes Summary

The Ordering and Registration Processes are the order fulfillment process that customers use to obtain the product/service offerings. It allows the customers to order, register, and participate in the product/service events that require registration for whatever reason.

AoP Summary

This Area of Performance is about

The formal Systems and Processes for addressing the Curriculum Manager's responsibilities in this Area of Performance include these nine processes:

- Master Materials Storage and Retrieval Processes
- Master Materials Change Management Processes
- Scheduling Processes
- Facilitator and Coach Development and Certification Processes
- Facilitator-led Content Deployment Processes
- Self-paced Content Deployment Processes
- Coached/Mentored Content Deployment Processes
- Individual Development Planning Processes
- Ordering and Registration Processes

The nine processes of the Product and Service Line Deployment System hold and maintain the L&D material masters, deploy/deliver the L&D from the supplier to the customer, and participate (except for some self-paced L&D) in the actual delivery activities (lectures, demos, and application exercises) and enable the advanced planning and ordering of content requiring that.

Part of your responsibility as a Curriculum Manager is to adopt and/ or adapt what has been presented here for your own context. Hopefully this has provided you with some guidance for doing that.

How Are You Currently Performing This Area of Performance Competence?

Regarding the Product and Service Line Deployment Area of Performance…

How are you currently **Planning this Work** – and how are you deciding what needs to get done, and by whom, and when?

What, if anything, needs to change?

How are you currently **Assigning this Work** – and how are you communicating the expectations of the work assignment?

What, if anything, needs to change?

How are you currently **Monitoring this Work** – and how are you focusing on the follow up monitoring of work processes and work products to insure that everything is okay?

What, if anything, needs to change?

How are you currently **Troubleshooting this Work** – and how are you following up for any work products or work processes where you spotted discrepancies, in order to resolve them?

What, if anything, needs to change?

Chapter Summary & Transition

This chapter was intended to address the processes of the Product and Service Line Deployment System.

This chapter logically leads to the next, but your needs may cause you to want to skip around.

The list of chapters and their pages numbers are presented next for your personal navigation needs and desires.

1	What Does a Curriculum Manager Do?	1
2	AoP: Stakeholder Needs Assessment & Alignment	27
3	AoP: Strategic Planning & Management	53
4	AoP: Operations Planning & Management	65
5	AoP: Results Measurement	79
6	AoP: Improvement Planning	95
7	AoP: Communications	107
8	AoP: Product & Service Line Design	120
9	AoP: Product & Service Line Development	143
10	AoP: Product & Service Line Deployment	169
11	AoP: Process Design & Redesign	193
12	AoP: Human Assets	203
13	AoP: Environmental Assets	222
14	AoP: Special Assignments	241

| 15 | Summary & Close | 247 |
| 16 | Additional Related Resources & References | 254 |

Suggested Chapter Reflection & Reaction

I would suggest that prior to jumping into whichever chapter meets your needs that you give pause for a moment to reflect on the following and make some notes:

- What are your own "ah-ha's" so far?

- Are the Deployment Processes you have in place adequate to your needs? If not, what is the cost of the problem or opportunity, and what are the potential Returns for any Investments for improving these?

- How would you need to think about this model differently than it is presented?

- What language changes and deletions or additions might you need to make?

- What are all of the implications for you and your L&D function thus far?

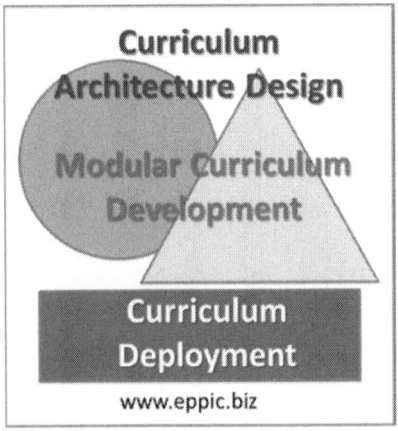

At the Core of a Curriculum Manager's
Performance Competence Requirements
are the architecture, development and deployment of
performance-enabling
Instructional and Informational Content

11 - AREA OF PERFORMANCE: PROCESS DESIGN & REDESIGN

Chapter Overview

Read or scan this chapter if you are concerned with:

- **Process Design & Redesign** – creating or improving the processes that are within your realm of responsibility.

This chapter is intended to provide you with some details related to this Area of Performance.

S1- Process Design/re-design – involves designing new processes and/or making changes to the existing processes in terms of their outputs, process flows, steps, inputs, individual contributors' roles and responsibilities, etc.

This chapter fits within the overall flow of the model as presented in the following graphic.

Curriculum Manager's Areas of Performance Competence Model

LEADERSHIP AoPs - Planning & Management
- Stakeholder Needs Assessment & Alignment
- Strategic Planning
- Operations Planning
- Results Measurement
- Improvement Planning
- Communications

CORE AoPs - Planning & Management
- Product & Service Line Design
- Product & Service Line Development
- Product & Service Line Deployment

SUPPORT AoPs - Planning & Management
- Process Design and Redesign
- Human Assets
- Environmental Assets
- Special Assignments

Adapted from the Management Areas of Performance Model
©2002 Guy W. Wallace

As you read through this chapter keep in mind your potential need to adapt this content to your context – or to adapt your context to this content.

AoP: S1- Process Design & Redesign

AoP Overview

The **Process Design/Re-design Area of Performance** involves the design or re-design of Enterprise processes within the scope of the Curriculum Manager, for processes they "own" and have authority over.

This **Support** AoP kicks into place when the executives of the Enterprise in conjunction with the appropriate manager decides that redesign (incremental or radical) of "their process" is called for, as a result of either their estimation of the "cost of conformance to Stakeholder metrics" or the "cost of non-conformance to Stakeholder metrics."

For a refresher on the "balancing of the various Stakeholders requirements," refer back to chapter 2.

Linked to this AoP are the **Leadership AoPs** of Improvement Planning & Management – covered in chapter 6. Plus this is linked to the Monitoring Work and Troubleshooting Work aspects of every AoP covered in this book… where you may have uncovered and then planned the need for any improvements – improvements that then need to be planned for and accomplished in this AoP of Process Design/Redesign.

AoP Typical Outputs

The Curriculum Manager's "**outputs**" for this Area of Performance might include:

- Process Re-design documentation which can include
    - Process maps
    - Value Stream maps, cost data
    - Performance models
    - Enabler Matrices for the human assets and environmental assets required
    - Policy (updates)
    - Methods & procedures (updates)
    - Specifications for new tools, materials, etc.
    - Etc.

AoP Typical Tasks

The "**tasks**" of this Area of Performance, related to the outputs above, might include:

- Mapping of the "current state/as is" process with a team of "master performers" from all portions of the current process
- Mapping of the "future state/to be" process with a team of
    - "Master performers" who are process participants in the "current-state" process and issues (problems/opportunities)
    - "Subject matter experts" who have knowledge/insight about any "future-state" issues
        - Future regulatory issues
        - Future policy issues
        - Future technology issues
        - Future competitive issues

- Collaborating with your "downstream customer representatives" who can represent the process output(s) users and ensure that their needs drive the output of the "future-state" process and help the process participants begin to determine the impact/feasibility and cost implications for any change requirements to their inputs to the "future-state" process
- Collaborating with your "upstream Supplier Representatives" who can represent the suppliers and begin to determine the impact/feasibility and cost implications for any change requirements to their inputs to the "future-state" process
- Developing all of the other documentation, per Enterprise standards/requirements/practice, or as locally determined as appropriate
- Communication/transmitting all new process documentation for review/approvals, or as inputs (as an FYI or to impact their activities and outputs) to other based on their "need to know"
- Developing an "Implementing Plan," and then immediately, or as quickly as possible/but as slowly as prudent, implementing the plan to make the changes
- All at once, or pilot testing as needed before a full roll-out

AoP Systems & Processes Overview
Next we will look at a formal System for addressing this AoP:

- **Process Design & Redesign**

The following Process of this System will be reviewed next:

- Process Design/Redesign

Process Design & Redesign Process

Process Purpose

To create an effective and efficient process or to improve an existing process so that they produce products (outputs) that meet all Stakeholder Requirements.

Process Description

This process starts with the end in mind and first defines the products or outputs of the process and determines the measures in terms of various factors within the categories of quality, quantity and costs.

Then the steps or activities are defined and the human and environmental support requirements are derived. After pilot-testing and post-pilot-testing updates and refinements are made it is implemented.

Is Your Process Design & Redesign Process Broken? Clues and Cues

Your Process Design & Redesign Process may be broken if:

- Processes designed, developed and implemented do not work as well as needed in producing the Products/ Outputs desired after improvement efforts.

Processes Summary

The Process Design & Redesign effort rationally conducts improvement initiatives and manages the project until done.

AoP Summary

This Area of Performance is about making improvements to the processes or creating new processes within the sphere responsibility and control of your as a Curriculum Manager.

Part of your responsibility as a Curriculum Manager is to adopt and/ or adapt what has been presented here for your own context. Hopefully this has provided you with some guidance for doing that.

How Are You Currently Performing This Area of Performance Competence?

How are you currently **Planning this Work** – and how are you deciding what needs to get done, and by whom, and when?

What, if anything, needs to change?

How are you currently **Assigning this Work** – and how are you communicating the expectations of the work assignment?

What, if anything, needs to change?

How are you currently **Monitoring this Work** – and how are you focusing on the follow up monitoring of work processes and work products to insure that everything is okay?

What, if anything, needs to change?

How are you currently **Troubleshooting this Work** – and how are you are following up for any work products or work processes where you spotted discrepancies, in order to resolve them?

What, if anything, needs to change?

Chapter Summary & Transition

This chapter was intended to address the Process Design and Redesign Areas of Performance of a Curriculum Manager.

This chapter logically leads to the next, but your needs may cause you to want to skip around.

The list of chapters and their pages numbers are presented next for your personal navigation needs and desires.

1	What Does a Curriculum Manager Do?	1
2	AoP: Stakeholder Needs Assessment & Alignment	27
3	AoP: Strategic Planning & Management	53
4	AoP: Operations Planning & Management	65
5	AoP: Results Measurement	79
6	AoP: Improvement Planning	95
7	AoP: Communications	107

8	AoP: Product & Service Line Design	120
9	AoP: Product & Service Line Development	143
10	AoP: Product & Service Line Deployment	169
11	AoP: Process Design & Redesign	193
12	AoP: Human Assets	203
13	AoP: Environmental Assets	222
14	AoP: Special Assignments	241
15	Summary & Close	247
16	Additional Related Resources & References	254

Suggested Chapter Reflection & Reaction

I would suggest that prior to jumping into whichever chapter meets your needs that you give pause for a moment to reflect on the following and make some notes:

- What are your own "ah-ha's" so far?

- Are the Processes you have in place for designing or redesigning processes adequate to your needs? If not, what is the cost of the problem or opportunity, and what are the potential Returns for any Investments for improving these?

- How would you need to think about this model differently than it is presented?

- What language changes and deletions or additions might you need to make?

- What are all of the implications for you and your L&D function thus far?

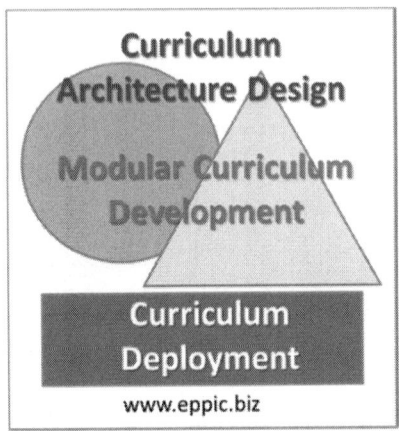

At the Core of a Curriculum Manager's
Performance Competence Requirements
are the architecture, development and deployment of
performance-enabling
Instructional and Informational Content

12 - AREA OF PERFORMANCE: HUMAN ASSETS

Chapter Overview

Read or scan this chapter if you are concerned with:

- **Human Assets** – which addresses the design of jobs and organizations, staff and career planning, recruiting and selection, training and development, performance appraisal and management, compensation and benefits, and rewards and recognition of your staff.

This chapter is intended to provide you with some details related to this Area of Performance (AoP).

S2- Human Assets – involves all aspects of job definition, and HR-type responsibilities for your staff.

This chapter fits within the overall flow of the model as presented in the following graphic.

Curriculum Manager's Areas of Performance Competence Model

LEADERSHIP AoPs - Planning & Management
- ☐ Stakeholder Needs Assessment & Alignment
- ☐ Strategic Planning
- ☐ Operations Planning
- ☐ Results Measurement
- ☐ Improvement Planning
- ☐ Communications

CORE AoPs - Planning & Management
- ☐ Product & Service Line Design
- ☐ Product & Service Line Development
- ☐ Product & Service Line Deployment

SUPPORT AoPs - Planning & Management
- ☐ Process Design and Redesign
- ☐ Human Assets
- ☐ Environmental Assets
- ☐ Special Assignments

Adapted from the Management Areas of Performance Model
©2002 Guy W. Wallace

As you read through this chapter keep in mind your potential need to adapt this content to your context – or to adapt your context to this content.

AoP: S2- Human Assets

AoP Overview

> The **Human Asset Planning & Management** Area of Performance involves doing the actual HR-type work or working in conjunction with HR personnel in the design of the jobs and the organizations, and then the planning and management of systems and processes/practices for staff planning and succession, recruiting and selection, training and development, assessment and performance management, compensation and benefits, and rewards and recognition – for all of the staff within your scope as the Curriculum Manager.

This is one of the more complex components of leadership and management performance for any manager – including the Curriculum Manager.

AoP Typical Outputs

The Curriculum Manager's "outputs" of this Area of Performance typically include:

Job and Organization Designs
- Which can include outputs such as updates or new items of-
    - Job descriptions and qualification requirements (per all legal and policy

- requirements/restrictions)
  - o Organization charts and reporting relationships
  - o Organization vision/mission/values statements

Staffing Plans
- Based on workload volumes and budget allocations/restrictions for headcount (or balancing the total expense budget) a plan is produced identifying the numbers of people in all jobs, for each planning period (annual, quarterly, monthly, weekly, daily . . . depending on the nature of the organization's work volumes and variation, seasonally driven or not) including both permanent employees and temporary employees. This plan would also identify the sources for the people (internal or external).

Succession Plans
- Based on the need to move people "up, over, or out" and with other "turnover," a plan for filling the staffing plan needs to be developed, identifying the sources internally (to create effective/efficient succession paths for employees seeking upward mobility) and external, and the timing for "bringing new people on board, and existing people into a new job" (per all legal and policy requirements/restrictions).

Recruiting Plans
- Based on the details and timing of the Successions Plans, a plan for recruiting (internally and externally) needs to be developed and implemented, including

the development and placement/dissemination of
- o Job postings/advertisements
- o Initial Screening mechanisms
  - Testing and review for various capabilities and issues (per all legal and policy requirements/restrictions)
    - Keyboard skills
    - Drug testing
    - Court/police records
    - Etc.

Selected Job Candidates

- Based on job candidate interviews and possibly further testing (per al legal and policy requirements/restriction), candidates are ranked for "making offers."

Job Offers

- Job offers (per all legal and policy requirements/restrictions) are made to candidates I the order of their previous ranking, including information regarding all compensation and benefits, etc. (per all legal and policy requirements/restrictions).

Orientation and Training

- For all "new employees" (either "new to the company" or "new to the job") who accepted the job offers, "Orientation and Training" plans are developed and implemented (per all legal and policy requirements/restrictions).

Performance Appraisals and Assessments

- Performance appraisals are done routinely and as needed, formally and informally (per all legal and policy requirements/restrictions) and documented as necessary. Decisions are made as to the appropriate response to any issues uncovered.

Disciplinary Actions
- Based on the appraisal or assessment of an individual (or teams) performance and any discrepancies uncovered, disciplinary action are considered (per all legal and policy requirements/restrictions). This "action" taken could include (per all legal and policy requirements/restrictions)
    o Counseling
    o Verbal warnings
    o Written warnings
    o Suspensions (with or without pay)
    o Termination

- Any disciplinary "action plan" might be created and reviewed with and agreed to by the employee (per all legal and policy requirements/restrictions).

Development Plans
- Per the assessments of performance and the determination of "root cause," if the "cause" is an awareness/knowledge/skill deficiency, training and development (via coaching, classroom, web, etc.) may be proscribed and implemented (per all legal and policy requirements/restrictions).

Compensation & Benefits Administration
- Based on the individual and/or team performance, compensation is administered (per all legal and policy requirements/restrictions), which could include
    o Allocation for "dollars" for raises, merit increases, bonuses, etc.

Rewards & Recognition
- Based on the individual and/or team performance, various rewards and recognition is administered (per all legal and policy requirements/restrictions), which could include
    - Small monetary reward
    - Large monetary rewards (sales contests)
    - Prizes
    - Public and private acknowledgements of "a job well done"
    - Etc.

AoP Typical Tasks

The "tasks" of this Area of Performance, related to the outputs above, typically include:

- Developing staffing plans
- Developing successions plans
- Developing recruiting plans
- Selecting job candidates to make offers to
- Making job offers
- Developing orientation and training plans and implementing them
- Conducting performance appraisals and assessments
- Taking disciplinary action as needed
- Developing and managing development plans
- Administering compensation & benefits
- Administering rewards & recognition systems and programs

Formal Processes of the AoP

The formal Processes of a Curriculum Manager's system to address this Area of Performance include:

- Staff Recruiting and Selection/Succession Processes
- Staff Training and Development Processes
- L&D Staff Assessment Processes
- L&D Staff Compensation and Benefits Processes
- L&D Staff Rewards and Recognition Processes

Let's start with Recruiting and Selection.

Staff Recruiting and Selection/Succession Processes

Processes Purpose

The Staff Recruiting and Selection/Succession Processes seek applicants and screens candidates for defined jobs/positions.

Processes Description

The Staff Recruiting and Selection/Succession Processes fill the organization chart with people for the various role/job responsibilities.

Once the processes have been articulated, and the workload volumes have been assessed, the staffing plan can be completed. This process fulfills the human asset requirements, whether via a permanent employee strategy, an outsourcing strategy, or a combination of the two.

Job management and team members, if appropriate, conduct the final selection evaluation for overall personal and organizational fit.

Are Your Staff Recruiting and Selection/Succession Processes Broken? Clues and Cues

Your Staff Recruiting and Selection/Succession Processes may be broken if:

- Your incoming staff members do not have the necessary entry knowledge and skills.
- Incoming staff have wildly varying incoming knowledge and skills.
- Existing staff are frequently not trainable or cannot be developed to competently meet the process requirements of the L&D systems and processes.
- Staff complains that the job was not what they expected (the real job requirements do not match job incumbents' incoming expectations).
- Staff is not brought on board in a timely manner.

Processes Summary

The Staff Recruiting and Selection/Succession Processes get the right people into the right jobs where they can be successful, either immediately or soon after any necessary development occurred to get them to where they need to be to be competent employees.

Next are the Processes for the staff development.

Staff Development Processes

Processes Purpose

The Staff Development Processes assess the knowledge and skill requirements and existing capabilities and then develops an Individual Development Plan for each of your staff members.

Processes Description

The Staff Development Processes "walks the talk," but not necessarily for everyone on the L&D staff.

We *never* subscribe to the notion that *everyone* should receive equal treatment regarding development. The owners/shareholders of the Enterprise simply cannot afford that philosophy and approach.

There are probably numerous others, better investments to make on behalf of the shareholders.

We subscribe to the plan to conduct L&D development projects for key, critical "PUSH" target audiences within the L&D processes, always consistent with the problems and opportunities within the L&D. This means first needs first, second-level needs second, and some needs never.

Are Your Staff Development Processes Broken? Clues and Cues

Your Staff Development Processes may be broken if:

- Your critical L&D staff is not as competent as they

need to be for knowledge/skills capability items outside the scope of the recruiting and selection process.
- Critical (PUSH) staff complains about the lack of L&D or lack of a clear path for their development.

Processes Summary

The Staff Development Processes ensure that key enabling knowledge/skills are developed for key roles/jobs within key processes.

Next, we'll look at assessing the individual performance of the L&D staff.

Staff Assessment Processes

Processes Purpose

The Staff Assessment Processes provide routine and continuous assessment of performance, positive/constructive feedback, negative/constructive feedback, additional development and progression monitoring, progressive discipline, and termination, if necessary.

Processes Description

The Staff Assessment Processes use the Enterprise's existing system (or its own) for appraising staff and providing feedback to the individual and/or team. It then provides "input" to the training and development process, the compensation and benefits process, and the rewards and recognition process.

Are Your Staff Assessment Processes Broken? Clues and Cues

Your Staff Assessment Processes may be broken if:

- Performance appraisals/staff evaluations don't happen routinely, or as needed, or with quality and consistency.
- The L&D staff does not know where they stand in management's eyes regarding their competence and performance adequacy.
- Staff L&D plans are not being driven by these formal assessments, which are driven by the needs of the business.
- Performance appraisals and criteria are too general and/or do not match the job.

Processes Summary

The Staff Assessment Processes ensure that the staff and their management are fully aware of their areas of strength and/or areas needing development.

Next are the compensation and benefits processes.

Staff Compensation and Benefits Processes

Processes Purpose

The Staff Compensation and Benefits Processes provide total compensation and benefits for all of the permanent employees of the L&D system; it typically provides only compensation for the outsourced staff.

Processes Description

The Staff Compensation and Benefits Processes ensure that local market conditions are reflected in the pay scales being used in each employment market within which the staff works. This process also includes the administration of various types of benefits including vacation, sick leave, etc.

Are Your Staff Compensation and Benefits Processes Broken? Clues and Cues

Your Staff Compensation and Benefits Processes may be broken if:

- The staff complains about their salary compared to others elsewhere in L&D.
- Pay is uneven across multiple jobs without solid rationale.
- Turnover is greater than in other areas of the Enterprise, and exit interviews indicate that people are leaving due to pay and benefits issues.

Processes Summary

The Staff Compensation and Benefits Processes ensure that the L&D staff is being compensated adequately given the job performance expected and the local market conditions.

Next, we'll cover rewards and recognition.

Staff Rewards and Recognition Processes

Processes Purpose

The Staff Rewards and Recognition Processes provide small monetary and other nonmonetary rewards and recognition to the staff, other non-staff, and various contributors to the overall L&D effort.

Processes Description

The Staff Rewards and Recognition Processes use small monetary and nonmonetary (noncash) rewards to reinforce certain behaviors and attitudes.

Examples of rewards and recognition could include

- Publicity in Enterprise paper and electronic publications/news organs
- Project commemoratives (paperweights, T-shirts, caps, golf umbrellas, pens, pencils, banners, photos, plaques, etc.)
- Press releases and photos sent to local newspapers, plus video clips sent to all local radio and TV stations (and national press if warranted)
- Two week-long professional conferences anywhere in Hawaii
- Bonuses and stock options
- Company car

Some of the above (e.g., company car) may be a component of the compensation and benefits system.

All of this must be administered fairly. The acknowledgment by the staff that the rewards and recognition process is fair is critical to its success.

Individuals, as well as teams, may be recognized for their efforts and/or results.

Failures (projects, not people) can also be recognized and "celebrated" and "promoted," but that is always done in an attempt to extinguish the key factors of the failure in order to stop it from reoccurring. Lessons learned come from both successes and failures.

Are Your Staff Rewards and Recognition Processes Broken? Clues and Cues

Your Staff Rewards and Recognition Processes may be broken if:

- No one ever or seldom receives rewards or recognition for jobs well done.
- The staff feels that the rewards and recognition are being awarded unfairly.

Processes Summary

The Staff Rewards and Recognition Processes use noncash and small monetary rewards to motivate and recognize the staff and all other participants in the overall L&D effort.

AoP Summary

This Area of Performance is about managing the Human Assets by providing your own processes with the humans who have the right assets, the right knowledge, skills, physical attributes, psychological attributes, intellectual assets, and values required by the processes of your L&D system.

The five processes supply all of the people assets (the human resources) needed in all of the L&D organization's processes and projects. Then they help manage them, develop them, assess their performance, develop them further, compensate them, and provide other rewards and recognition. These five processes involve the Curriculum Manager who typically gets support and guidance from the Human Resources department.

The five formal Systems and Processes for addressing the Curriculum Manager's responsibilities include:

- Staff Recruiting and Selection/Succession Processes
- Staff Training and Development Processes
- L&D Staff Assessment Processes
- L&D Staff Compensation and Benefits Processes
- L&D Staff Rewards and Recognition Processes

Part of your responsibility as a Curriculum Manager is to adopt and/ or adapt what has been presented here for your own context. Hopefully this has provided you with some guidance for doing that.

How Are You Currently Performing This Area of Performance Competence?

How are you currently **Planning this Work** – and how are you deciding what needs to get done, and by whom, and when?

What, if anything, needs to change?

How are you currently **Assigning this Work** – and how are you communicating the expectations of the work assignment?

What, if anything, needs to change?

How are you currently **Monitoring this Work** – and how are you focusing on the follow up monitoring of work processes and work products to insure that everything is okay?

What, if anything, needs to change?

How are you currently **Troubleshooting Work** – and how are you following up for any work products or work processes where you spotted discrepancies, in order to resolve them?

What, if anything, needs to change?

Chapter Summary & Transition

This chapter was intended to address managing the Human Assets, the people of the L&D organization.

This chapter logically leads to the next, but your needs may cause you to want to skip around.

The list of chapters and their pages numbers are presented next for your personal navigation needs and desires.

1	What Does a Curriculum Manager Do?	1
2	AoP: Stakeholder Needs Assessment & Alignment	27
3	AoP: Strategic Planning & Management	53
4	AoP: Operations Planning & Management	65

5	AoP: Results Measurement	79
6	AoP: Improvement Planning	95
7	AoP: Communications	107
8	AoP: Product & Service Line Design	120
9	AoP: Product & Service Line Development	143
10	AoP: Product & Service Line Deployment	169
11	AoP: Process Design & Redesign	193
12	AoP: Human Assets	203
13	AoP: Environmental Assets	222
14	AoP: Special Assignments	241
15	Summary & Close	247
16	Additional Related Resources & References	254

Suggested Chapter Reflection & Reaction

I would suggest that prior to jumping into whichever chapter meets your needs that you give pause for a moment to reflect on the following and make some notes:

- What are your own "ah-ha's" so far?

- Are the Human Asset Management Processes that you have in place adequate to your needs? If not, what is the cost of the problem or opportunity, and what are the potential Returns for any Investments for improving these?

- How would you need to think about this model differently than it is presented?

- What language changes and deletions or additions might you need to make?

- What are all of the implications for you and your L&D function thus far?

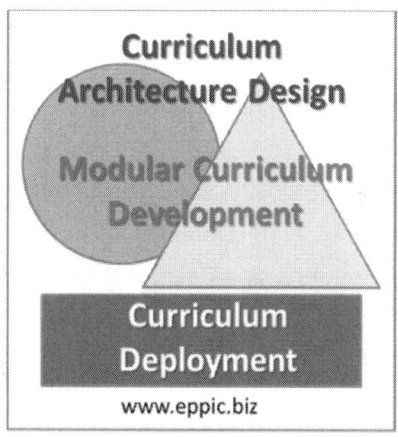

At the Core of a Curriculum Manager's
Performance Competence Requirements
are the architecture, development and deployment of
performance-enabling
Instructional and Informational Content

13 - AREA OF PERFORMANCE: ENVIRONMENTAL ASSETS

Chapter Overview

Read or scan this chapter if you are concerned with:

- **Environmental Assets** – the acquisition and development and maintenance of the non-human assets necessary as driven to the process requirements.

This chapter is intended to provide you with some details related to this Area of Performance and the acquisition/

development/maintenance of any and all of the "non-human" assets necessary to the process, including: data/ information, materials/ supplies, tools/ equipment, financial/ headcount, facilities/ grounds, culture/ consequences.

This chapter fits within the overall flow of the model as presented in the following graphic.

Curriculum Manager's Areas of Performance Competence Model

LEADERSHIP AoPs - Planning & Management
- ❑ Stakeholder Needs Assessment & Alignment
- ❑ Strategic Planning
- ❑ Operations Planning
- ❑ Results Measurement
- ❑ Improvement Planning
- ❑ Communications

CORE AoPs - Planning & Management
- ❑ Product & Service Line Design
- ❑ Product & Service Line Development
- ❑ Product & Service Line Deployment

SUPPORT AoPs - Planning & Management
- ❑ Process Design and Redesign
- ❑ Human Assets
- ❑ Environmental Assets
- ❑ Special Assignments

Adapted from the Management Areas of Performance Model
©2002 Guy W. Wallace

As you read through this chapter keep in mind your potential need to adapt this content to your context – or to adapt your context to this content.

AoP: S3- Environmental Asset

AoP Overview

Environmental Asset involves the planning for, acquisition of, implementation of, and the on-going assessment of all of the non-human/environmental assets required by all of your Processes, within the scope of the Curriculum Manager's job.

This is also one of the more complex components of leadership and management performance.

Typical Outputs

The Curriculum Manager's "**outputs**" for this Area of Performance typically include:

Relevant **Data and Information** made available for yourself and for your subordinates to support your/their work performance requirements, including-
- Job Descriptions/expectations
- Policies
- Procedures/process guidelines
- Work orders
- Customer feedback
- Process performance results data
- Quality results data

- Quantity results data
- Cost results data
- Cycle time results data
- Etc.

Materials and Supplies made available for yourself and for your subordinates to support your/their work performance requirements, including-
- Raw goods/end product components
- Process consumables
- Flip chart easel paper
- Etc.

Tools and Equipment made available for yourself and for your subordinates to support your/their work performance requirements, including-
- Flip chart easels
- Computers
- Software/applications
- Machinery
- Vehicles
- Etc.

Facilities and Grounds made available for yourself and for your subordinates to support your/their work performance requirements, including-
- Buildings
- Parking facilities
- Storage facilities
- Furniture
- Utilities
  - Electrical
  - Water
  - Gas

    o   Phone lines
- Etc.

Budget and Headcount made available for yourself and for your subordinates to support your/their work performance requirements, including-
- Expense budgets
    o   Utilities
    o   Supplies
    o   Overtime
- Capital budgets
- Headcount budgets
- Etc.

Culture and Consequences, as appropriate made available for yourself and for your subordinates to support your/their work performance requirements, including -
- Openness/trust
- Empowerment/Engagement practices
- Risk tolerance/acceptance/encouragement
- Etc.

Typical Tasks

The "**tasks**" of this Area of Performance, related to the outputs above, typically include:

- Determine the process' feedback/measuring/monitoring data requirements
- Set up systems, or otherwise obtain the data needed in a user-friendly configuration to achieve the process performance objectives
- Determine the process performance material and supply requirements
- Set up systems or otherwise obtain the material and supply needed to achieve the process performance

objectives
- Determine the process performance tools/equipment requirements
- Obtain/acquire the tools/equipment needed to achieve the process performance objectives
- Determine the process performance facilities and grounds requirements
- Obtain/acquire the facilities and grounds needed to achieve the process performance objectives
- Determine the process performance budget and headcount requirements
- Obtain/acquire the budget and headcount needed to achieve the process performance objectives
- Determine the process performance culture and consequence requirements
- Set up systems, or otherwise implement the culture and consequence systems needed to achieve the process performance objectives

Formal Processes of the AoP

The Environmental Asset System provides all of the infrastructure and resources needed by the humans involved in the L&D systems.

The six formal Processes of the Environmental Assets system to address this Area of Performance include:

- Organization Structural Design Processes
- Facilities Development and Deployment Processes
- Equipment and Tools Development and Deployment Processes
- Materials and Supplies Acquisition and Deployment Processes
- Information Systems Development and

Deployment Processes
- Methods Deployment Processes

Let's start.

Organization Structural Design Processes

Processes Purpose

The Organization Structural Design Processes design the organization (the form and structure) based on the leadership, core, and support processes in place and the systems, tools, and methods required to render the products and services that have high-payback to the Enterprise in terms of their Returns on Investments – or Economic Value Add.

Processes Description

The Organization Structural Design Processes design the organization and jobs required to carry out the work of the L&D system, as articulated in the L&D systems and processes specifics. Form should follow function.

Many L&D organization designs and the job designs within have evolved over time and were not necessarily designed to meet all of today's current requirements. They need to be re-engineered from a process performance perspective.

Are Your Environmental Asset Management Processes Broken? Clues and Cues

Your Organization Structural Design Processes may be broken if:

- Job responsibilities overlap or are gapped.
- Organization responsibilities overlap or are gapped.
- Staff, management, and/or customers do not know who does what.

Processes Summary

The Organization Structural Design Processes ensure a sound process performance orientation to the design of each job that is needed to carry out the specific work required in the L&D organization's Process and Practices, and their unique and common needs.

Next, we'll view the Processes for facilities development and deployment.

Facilities Development and Deployment Processes

Processes Purpose

The Facilities Development and Deployment Processes build or acquire and maintain all of the facilities (buildings and grounds) needed by L&D.

Processes Description

The Facilities Development and Deployment Processes will be driven by the method for L&D deployment, the number of staff members, the locations of where L&D will do its business, and the responsibilities for those locations.

If every L&D product was intended to be delivered electronically to the desktop (heaven and shareholders forbid!), then there wouldn't be a need for classrooms, just space for the developers and administrators to sit. A more likely scenario will require a blend of facility types.

This process may be owned by another Enterprise/corporate group, but this L&D process ensures that L&D -specific input is provided to the owning organization, in order to ensure that form follows function (both current-state function and near-term, future-state function).

Are Your Facility Development and Deployment Processes Broken? Clues and Cues

Your Facilities Development and Deployment Processes may be broken if:

- Your space needs are not being met.
- Your space is not conducive to what you are doing and how you are doing it.
- There is no short- and/or long-term, strategically driven view of what those needs are or will be.

Processes Summary

The Facilities Development and Deployment Processes attempt to forecast the needs of the L&D system for facilities that will be conducive to current needs and robust (flexible) to future needs.

Next, we'll look at the equipment and tools required.

Equipment and Tools Development and Deployment Processes

Processes Purpose

The Equipment and Tools Development and Deployment Processes build or acquire the tools and equipment required and proven (pilot tested) by the research and development effort. This process ensures a successful implementation.

Processes Description

The Equipment and Tools Development and Deployment Processes determine the equipment and tool needs based on the systems' processes and the job designs for performing within those processes.

These tools and equipment can include various types of furniture, presentation equipment, computers and peripherals, etc.

Are Your Equipment Development and Deployment Processes Broken? Clues and Cues

Your Equipment and Tools Development and Deployment Processes may be broken if:

- The equipment and tools required to get the job done are lacking (totally, or in the correct quantity) or are otherwise inadequate for the tasks of the processes.
- There are budget overruns and high costs for outsourcing and/or last-minute expediting.

Processes Summary

The Equipment and Tools Development and Deployment Processes put in place all of the equipment and tools needed by the L&D system.

Next, we'll cover the L&D Materials and Supplies Acquisition and Deployment Processes.

Materials and Supplies Acquisition and Deployment Processes

Processes Purpose

The Materials and Supplies Acquisition and Deployment Processes acquire and deliver all consumable materials and supplies necessary for L&D operations.

Processes Description

The Materials and Supplies Acquisition and Deployment Processes ensure that the material and supply needs of the L&D system are being met.

Are Your Material and Supplies Acquisition and Deployment Processes Broken? Clues and Cues

Your Materials and Supplies Acquisition and Deployment Processes may be broken if:

- Materials and supplies constantly run out.
- Incorrect materials and supplies are ordered and inventoried.
- You are over-stocked too often.
- Costs paid for materials and supplies too often include expediting charges for rush orders.

Processes Summary

The Materials and Supplies Acquisition and Deployment Processes ensure that the materials and supply needs of the L&D system are met.

Next, we'll look at the L&D Information Systems Development and Deployment Processes.

Information Systems Development and Deployment Processes

Processes Purpose

The Information Systems Development and Deployment Processes build or acquire the L&D information technology methods and systems (hardware and software) that are deemed required and have been proven (pilot tested) by L&D research and development effort to meet their intended functionality.

Processes Description

The Information Systems Development and Deployment Processes ensure that the information capture, archiving, and deployment needs of the L&D system are capable. This process ensures a successful information technology (IT) or information system (IS) implementation.

Everything today is bits and bytes: data. Powerful systems exist to capture, store, and report this data. Communications networks exist to deploy data and courseware and other e-learning approaches such as Knowledge Management Systems, wikis, and a host of other brand and generic names that will drive this need to a higher level than ever before.

Even with a blended strategy (using both electronic and traditional deployment methods), the IT/IS systems can quickly and cheaply deploy the group-paced facilitator materials across the globe to wherever the facilitator is.

Are Your Information Systems Development and Deployment Processes Broken? Clues and Cues

Your Information Systems Development and Deployment Processes may be broken if:

- The current IT/IS system is inadequate to the task, from space (storage size) to speed (computational power and bandwidth in the distribution pipes).
- There is no near-term or long-range plan for the IT/IS system.

Processes Summary

The Information Systems Development and Deployment Processes ensure that the IT or IS systems will meet the current, near-term, and long-term needs of the L&D system.

Next, we'll look at the L&D Methods Deployment Processes.

Methods Deployment Processes

Processes Purpose

The Methods Deployment Processes builds or acquires the L&D and administrative methods that have been tested and or are part of Enterprise-wide methods and procedures.

These processes ensure an overall, successful implementation of any new approaches to ISD or other L&D processes, practices and methods.

Processes Description

The Methods Deployment Processes address procedures/methods for conducting various L&D processes such as L&D development, vendor selection, expense reimbursement, L&D material updates, internal communications, etc.

These methods are derived from and are in sync with the overall L&D systems' processes views and the process maps and Performance Models that describe the details of each.

Are Your Methods Deployment Processes Broken? Clues and Cues

Your Methods Deployment Processes may be broken if:

- You don't have methods documented for key process performance tasks.
- Variation in how things are done is causing problems with consistency in quality, cost, or schedule performance.

Processes Summary

The Methods Deployment Processes provide guidance in critical tasks to ensure better quality and cost and schedule performance.

AoP Summary

This Area of Performance is about the Systems and Processes that provide all of the process infrastructure needed by the humans involved in the L&D systems.

The six formal Systems and Processes for addressing the Curriculum Manager's responsibilities include

- Organization Structural Design Processes
- Facilities Development and Deployment Processes
- Equipment and Tools Development and Deployment Processes
- Materials and Supplies Acquisition and Deployment Processes
- Information Systems Development and Deployment Processes
- Methods Deployment Processes

Part of your responsibility as a Curriculum Manager is to adopt and/ or adapt what has been presented here for your own context. Hopefully this has provided you with some guidance for doing that.

How Are You Currently Performing This Area of Performance Competence?

How are you currently **Planning this Work** – and how are you deciding what needs to get done, and by whom, and when?

What, if anything, needs to change?

How are you currently **Assigning this Work** – and how are you communicating the expectations of the work assignment?

What, if anything, needs to change?

How are you currently **Monitoring this Work** – and how are you focusing on the follow up monitoring of work processes and work products to insure that everything is okay?

What, if anything, needs to change?

How are you currently **Troubleshooting this Work** – and how are you following up for any work products or work processes where you spotted discrepancies, in order to resolve them?

What, if anything, needs to change?

Chapter Summary & Transition

This chapter was intended to address the Environmental Assets and the Systems and Processes needed by the humans involved in the L&D systems.

This chapter logically leads to the next, but your needs may cause you to want to skip around.

The list of chapters and their pages numbers are presented next for your personal navigation needs and desires.

1   What Does a Curriculum Manager Do?   1

2	AoP: Stakeholder Needs Assessment & Alignment	27
3	AoP: Strategic Planning & Management	53
4	AoP: Operations Planning & Management	65
5	AoP: Results Measurement	79
6	AoP: Improvement Planning	95
7	AoP: Communications	107
8	AoP: Product & Service Line Design	120
9	AoP: Product & Service Line Development	143
10	AoP: Product & Service Line Deployment	169
11	AoP: Process Design & Redesign	193
12	AoP: Human Assets	203
13	AoP: Environmental Assets	222
14	AoP: Special Assignments	241
15	Summary & Close	247
16	Additional Related Resources & References	254

Suggested Chapter Reflection & Reaction

I would suggest that prior to jumping into whichever chapter meets your needs that you give pause for a moment to reflect on the following and make some notes:

- What are your own "ah-ha's" so far?

- Are the Environmental Asset Processes you have in place adequate to your needs? If not, what is the cost of the problem or opportunity, and what are the potential Returns for any Investments for improving these?

- How would you need to think about this model differently than it is presented?

- What language changes and deletions or additions might you need to make?

- What are all of the implications for you and your L&D function thus far?

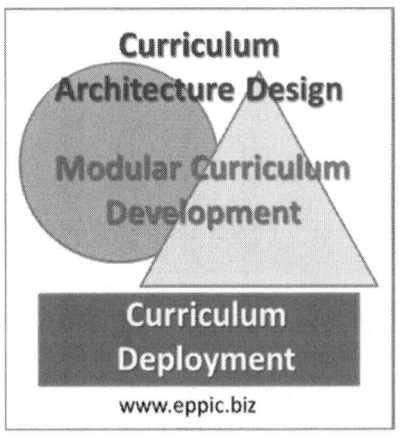

At the Core of a Curriculum Manager's
Performance Competence Requirements
are the architecture, development and deployment of performance-enabling
Instructional and Informational Content

14 - AREA OF PERFORMANCE: SPECIAL ASSIGNMENTS

Chapter Overview

Read this short chapter if you have:

- **Special Assignments** – otherwise known as: "other duties as assigned."

This short chapter is a catch all – one where you may capture some or all of the unique aspects of your job as a Curriculum Manager.

This chapter fits within the overall flow of the model as presented in the following graphic.

Curriculum Manager's Areas of Performance Competence Model

LEADERSHIP AoPs - Planning & Management
- ❑ Stakeholder Needs Assessment & Alignment
- ❑ Strategic Planning
- ❑ Operations Planning
- ❑ Results Measurement
- ❑ Improvement Planning
- ❑ Communications

CORE AoPs - Planning & Management
- ❑ Product & Service Line Design
- ❑ Product & Service Line Development
- ❑ Product & Service Line Deployment

SUPPORT AoPs - Planning & Management
- ❑ Process Design and Redesign
- ❑ Human Assets
- ❑ Environmental Assets
- ❑ Special Assignments

Adapted from the Management Areas of Performance Model
©2002 Guy W. Wallace

AoP: S4- Special Assignments

This Area of Performance is completely unique to you and your context.

You might wish to spend a little time thinking about the "other duties as assigned" aspects of your current job as a Curriculum Manager. Perhaps these other duties are distracting you from more important work, and you'll need to make a case to hand them off to some other job.

Part of your responsibility as a Curriculum Manager is to adopt and/ or adapt what has been presented here for your own context.

However, I am unable to provide you with much guidance for doing that for this AoP. You are on your own.

Perhaps you support other department's cross-functional Processes, perhaps not. It's things like that – that are taking up your time and energy – and keeping you from the aspects of a Curriculum Manager's job as I've defined it here.

So – if you have other duties as assigned, make note of them now. What are they, what outputs and tasks are involved? Should these be handed-off to someone else? Who?

The following wraps this AoP up…

How Are You Currently Performing This Area of Performance Competence?

How are you currently **Planning this Work** – and how are you deciding what needs to get done, and by whom, and when?

What, if anything, needs to change?

How are you currently **Assigning this Work** – and how are you communicating the expectations of the work assignment?

What, if anything, needs to change?

How are you currently **Monitoring this Work** – and how are you focusing on the follow up monitoring of work processes and products to insure that everything is okay?

What, if anything, needs to change?

How are you currently **Troubleshooting this Work** – and how are you following up for any work products or work processes where you have spotted discrepancies, in order to resolve them?

What, if anything, needs to change?

Chapter Summary & Transition

This chapter was intended to address the aspects of your assignment as a Curriculum Manager that are not covered directly in this book.

This chapter leads to the book summary.

You may have been skipping around the chapters – and reading them in a sequence different that presented.

Check the chapters below to complete your personal navigation of the book's content.

| 1 | What Does a Curriculum Manager Do? | 1 |
| 2 | AoP: Stakeholder Needs Assessment & | 27 |

	Alignment	
3	AoP: Strategic Planning & Management	53
4	AoP: Operations Planning & Management	65
5	AoP: Results Measurement	79
6	AoP: Improvement Planning	95
7	AoP: Communications	107
8	AoP: Product & Service Line Design	120
9	AoP: Product & Service Line Development	143
10	AoP: Product & Service Line Deployment	169
11	AoP: Process Design & Redesign	193
12	AoP: Human Assets	203
13	AoP: Environmental Assets	222
14	AoP: Special Assignments	241
15	Summary & Close	247
16	Additional Related Resources & References	254

Suggested Chapter Reflection & Reaction

I would suggest that prior to jumping into whichever chapter meets your needs that you give pause for a moment to reflect on the following and make some notes:

- What are your own "ah-ha's" so far?

- Are the Processes for all of your Special Assignments in place and adequate to your needs? If not what is the cost of the problem or opportunity, and what are the potential Returns for any Investments for improving these?

- How would you need to think about this model differently than it is presented?

- What language changes and deletions or additions might you need to make?

- What are all of the implications for you and your L&D function thus far?

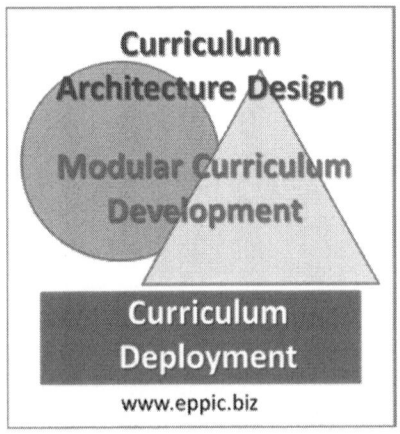

At the Core of a Curriculum Manager's
Performance Competence Requirements
are the architecture, development and deployment of
performance-enabling
Instructional and Informational Content

15 – SUMMARY & CLOSE

Chapter Overview

This chapter wraps up the book with a summary and close.

Book Summary & Transition

We have covered the following:

- **What Does a Curriculum Manager Do?**
  Although job titles may vary – we presented the following AoPs (Areas of Performance) as the framework for defining your role as a Curriculum manager.

- AoP: **Stakeholder Needs Assessment & Alignment**. This is the most critical aspect of your role – getting aligned to the priorities of your Customers and other Stakeholders. This can be done formally – or informally.

- AoP: **Strategic Planning & Management**. Getting yourself and your organization ready for the future while attending to the present may be tricky – but it is necessary. Document these so that you can share them in your collaboration with your Customers and Stakeholders.

- AoP: **Operations Planning & Management**. Getting a handle on your plans and budgets for the current year is necessary if you hope to actually achieve the goals and plans everyone else has for you. Document these so that you can share them in your collaboration with your Customers and Stakeholders.

- AoP: **Results Measurement**. Measure what is important to your Customers and Stakeholders using their business metrics, not Learning Metrics.

- AoP: **Improvement Planning**. Plan to improve where it makes sense and makes you a more effective and efficient steward of shareholder equity.

- AoP: **Communications**. This is where you would plan for both proactive and reactive communications for some or all of your key Stakeholders.

- AoP: **Product & Service Line Design**. This is where both a Portfolio Plan and a Curriculum

Architecture Design is done for the most critical of your Target Audiences.

- AoP: **Product & Service Line Development**. This is where you use an ADDIE-like approach to new product (and service) development.

- AoP: **Product & Service Line Deployment**. This is where you deliberately look at the systems you have in place to deploy – and/or make accessible – your products and services.

- AoP: **Process Design & Redesign**. This is where you document existing processes, create new ones, or improve old ones that need it (but only if there is enough R for the I).

- AoP: **Human Assets**. This is where you put all of the human resources (assets) into place to bring your paper processes to life.

- AoP: **Environmental Assets**. This is where you put everything else in place to assist your human resources (assets) in bringing your paper processes to life.

- AoP: **Special Assignments**. This is a catch all – but it would be good for you to have documented these "other duties" as they may be hindering your effectiveness in your Curriculum Manager role.

We followed this framework for the above content.

Curriculum Manager's Areas of Performance Competence Model

LEADERSHIP AoPs - Planning & Management
- ❑ Stakeholder Needs Assessment & Alignment
- ❑ Strategic Planning
- ❑ Operations Planning
- ❑ Results Measurement
- ❑ Improvement Planning
- ❑ Communications

CORE AoPs - Planning & Management
- ❑ Product & Service Line Design
- ❑ Product & Service Line Development
- ❑ Product & Service Line Deployment

SUPPORT AoPs - Planning & Management
- ❑ Process Design and Redesign
- ❑ Human Assets
- ❑ Environmental Assets
- ❑ Special Assignments

Adapted from the Management Areas of Performance Model
©2002 Guy W. Wallace

That concludes this book – other than some additional resources and references in the next and final chapter.

Your needs may have caused you to skip around and read this book in some other sequence than presented.

Check the list of chapters and their pages numbers below to complete your personal navigation needs and desires.

1	What Does a Curriculum Manager Do?	1
2	AoP: Stakeholder Needs Assessment & Alignment	27
3	AoP: Strategic Planning & Management	53
4	AoP: Operations Planning & Management	65
5	AoP: Results Measurement	79
6	AoP: Improvement Planning	95
7	AoP: Communications	107
8	AoP: Product & Service Line Design	120
9	AoP: Product & Service Line Development	143
10	AoP: Product & Service Line Deployment	169
11	AoP: Process Design & Redesign	193
12	AoP: Human Assets	203
13	AoP: Environmental Assets	222
14	AoP: Special Assignments	241
15	Summary & Close	247
16	Additional Related Resources & References	254

Suggested Book Reflection & Reaction

I would suggest that prior to putting this book down and away – that you give pause for a few moments to reflect on everything that you have read, and the previous notes that you have made, and then summarize your notes in one place:

- What are your own "ah-ha's" now that you have completed this book?

- How would you need to think about this model differently than it is presented?

- What language changes and deletions or additions might you really need to make?

- What are all of the implications for you and your organization?

- What will you do with this – and when will you start – and who else might you involve?

- Who else should I share this book with and encourage them to read it? Should they read selected portions, or should they read the whole thing?

Now your work really begins. Decide what you need to focus on – make a plan and then flexibly implement that plan.

Thank you for reading this book!

And best wishes in your role as a Curriculum Manager!

# # #

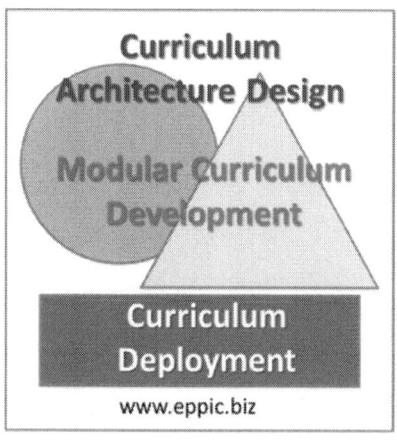

At the Core of a Curriculum Manager's
Performance Competence Requirements
are the architecture, development and deployment of
performance-enabling
Instructional and Informational Content

16 – ADDITIONAL RELATED RESOURCES & REFERENCES

Chapter Overview

This chapter is intended to provide you with additional **Resources and References** to help you further with your analysis and post–analysis efforts.

These are not just of general interest – that ocean is too large to boil down into a few cups of relevancy.

These resources and references relate specifically to what has been covered in this book.

Resources and References

Books

Improving Performance: How to manage the white space on the organization chart. (1990) by Geary A. Rummler and Alan Brache

The late Dr. Rummler was a friend and a mentor, going back to 1980. I had the pleasure of working with him on a half dozen or so projects when I was at Motorola 1981–1982 – and in interacting with him on client projects in the late 1990s and early 2000s. We also worked together in an attempt to clarify Human Performance Technology for our professional society back in 2003-2004.

My methods and the data I suggest capturing are actually derivatives of derivatives of his work when he co-led The Praxis Corporation in the 1970s with Tom Gilbert – which I learned in 1979. Any fault with these methods is attributed to me and certainly not to him.

Beyond the Myths and Magic of Mentoring: How to Facilitate an Effective Mentoring Process (2001) by Margo Murray.

This book provides guidance for determining organizational readiness and for structuring the roles and processes necessary for success.

The Quality RoadMap. (1994) by Ray Svenson, Karen Kennedy and Guy Wallace

This book is now out of print – but available at times as a used book. It presents a Business Architecture that we, the partners at SWI – Svenson & Wallace Inc. had developed and evolved and used in our consulting practices going back 10 years earlier. The book reflects our processes, practices and methods as used on a project with the Council for Continuous Improvement in the early 1990s.

Lean–ISD (1999) by Guy W. Wallace

ISD is an acronym for Instructional Systems Design. This book is available as a hardbound, a Kindle and as a free 404-page PDF at www.eppic.biz. It covers the analysis of the enabling knowledge and skills in great detail and the down-steam applications of that data in Curriculum Architecture Design efforts as well as in Content development efforts.

This book was the recipient of an Award of Excellence from the International Society for Performance Improvement in 2002.

L&D Systems View (2001) by Guy W. Wallace

This book is available as a hardbound, a Kindle and as a free PDF at www.eppic.biz. It covers the enabling Human and Environmental Assets as needed in a Training & Development or Learning & Development function/department.

Management Areas of Performance (2007) by Guy W. Wallace

This book is available as a free PDF at www.eppic.biz. It covers the Management Areas of Performance Model as a diagnostic tool and planning tool for Management Development for one's self and one's management staff.

Employee Performance-based Qualification/ Certification Systems (2008) by Ray Svenson & Guy W. Wallace

This book is available as a free PDF at www.eppic.biz. It covers the development of Performance Tests using the kind of analysis data presented in the Analysis of Performance Competence Requirements book.

Other books by Guy W. Wallace

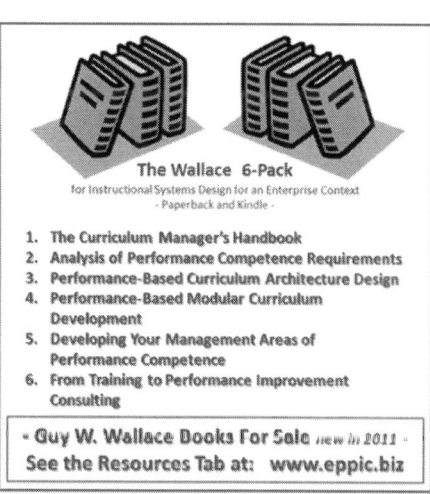

Handbook of Human Performance Technology - Chapter 11: Modeling Mastery Performance and Systematically Deriving the Enablers for Performance Improvement (2006) by Guy W. Wallace. This chapter covers the basics of modeling performance and deriving the enablers.

Analysis of Performance Competence Requirements (2011) by Guy W. Wallace

This book is available both a paperback and as a Kindle book via www.eppic.biz. It covers the analysis of Performance Competence Requirements using many of the same models presented in this book.

Article

The following Article relates directly to the content of this book.

The Customer is King...Not! : Balancing Conflicting Stakeholder Requirements

Copyright: 1995, AQP - Author: Wallace, Guy W. - Journal for Quality and Participation, Vol. 18, No. 2, March 1995, pp. 84-89.

This article articulates the various Stakeholder groups and presents a Stakeholder Requirements Matrix development instructions and an example.

Newsletter Articles

The following are a few of relevant Newsletter articles from over 10 years of publications – all available at www.eppic.biz

– in the Resources Tab. Search them all using the titles here - or key words and phrases from this book.

Wallace, G.W. (2000) **The AoP Framework for Management**. Lean–ISD Newsletter, (3)1, 1,7. CADDI: Naperville: CADDI Inc.

Wallace, G.W. (2000) **L&D Systems View– 10 and 11 O' Clock.** Lean–ISD Newsletter, (3)4, 19–22. CADDI: Naperville: CADDI Inc.

Wallace, G.W. (2000) **Human Asset Management Planning & Management.** Lean–ISD Newsletter, (3)4, 27–27. CADDI: Naperville: CADDI Inc.

Wallace, G.W. (2000) **Environmental Asset Management Planning & Management**. Lean–ISD Newsletter (3)5, 43–43. CADDI: Naperville: CADDI Inc.

This book was intended to help you with the

...the means to the ends of ...

ABOUT THE AUTHOR

Guy W. Wallace has been in the performance improvement field since 1979 and has been an external consultant to government and industry since 1982. His clients since then have included more than 60 firms, with over 40 Fortune 500 firms; plus he has worked with NASA, NAVSEA, NAVAIR, the NSA, BP, Opel, and Siemen's Building Technologies.

He has analyzed, designed, and developed improvement interventions, including job and organizational designs, recruiting and selection systems, training and development, pay–for–performance systems for a wide variety of industries and business functions and processes.

He is the author/ co–author of 9 books, several chapters, and more than 90 published articles beginning in 1984. Since 1982 he has presented more than 90 times at international conferences and local chapters of the International Society for Performance Improvement (ISPI), the American Society for Training & Development (ASTD), plus he has spoken at Training Magazine's Lakewood Conferences, the Association for Behavior Analysis (ABA), and the Conference on Nuclear Training & Education.

Guy W. Wallace served on the ISPI's executive committee as the treasurer for the 1999–2001 boards and as ISPI's president–elect and then president for 2002–2004.

His professional biography was listed in Who's Who in America in 2001 and he was designated a Certified Performance Technologist in 2002.

He received ISPI's highest honorary award, the Honorary Member for Life Award for his contributions to both the Society and to the technology of Human Performance Technology (HPT) in 2010.

He was also recruited as an inaugural member of the American Society for Quality's (ASQ) Influential Voices campaign in 2010.

Guy's consulting clients between 1982–2010 – and the number of engagements he performed for each client is presented next.

Abbott Laboratories (3) – ALCOA (2) – ALCOA Labs (2) – Alyeska Pipeline Services Company (2) – American Management Systems (1) – Ameritech (1) – Amoco Corporation (13) – Arthur Andersen (1) – ARCO of Alaska (3) – AT&T (4) – AT&T Communications (1) – AT&T Microelectronics (1) – AT&T Network Systems (24)

Bandag (7) – Bank of America (2) – Baxter (1) – Bellcore Tech (1) – British Petroleum–America (1) – Burroughs (1) – Channel Gas Industries/ Tenneco (1) – Commerce Clearing House (1) – Data General (1) – Detroit Ball Bearing (1) – Digital Equipment Corporation (2) – Discover Card (1) – Dow Chemical (3) – EDS (1) – Eli Lilly (7) – Exxon Exploration (2)

Fireman's Fund Insurance (1) – Ford Design Institute (1) – Ford Motor Company (1) – General Dynamics (10) – General Motors (25) – GTE (1) – H&R Block (1) – Hewlett Packard (5) – Illinois Bell (3) – Imperial Bondware (1) – Imperial Oil (1) – Johnson Controls (1) – Kodak (1) – Lockheed (1) – MCC Powers (16) – Motorola (1) – Multigraphics (1)

NASA (1) – NASCO (1) – NAVAIR (1) – NAVSEA (2) – NCR (2) – Norfolk Naval Shipyard (4) – Northern Telecom (1) – Northern Trust Bank (1) – NOVA (2) – NSA (1) – Opel (1) – Occidental Petroleum Labs (1) – Pacific Gas & Electric (1) – Quaker (1) – Siemens Building Technologies (1) – Spartan Stores (1) – Sphinx Pharmaceuticals (1) – Square D Company (2) – SunTrust Banks (2) – Valuemetrics (1) – Verizon (3) – Verizon Information Services (1) – Wells Fargo Advisors (1) – Westinghouse Defense Electronics (1)

Overviews for each of the projects above may be found on his web site at: www.eppic.biz

LinkedIn Reference

Richard E. Clark, PhD – USC
Professor and Director, Center for Cognitive Technology, University of Southern California — clark@usc.edu

Dick Clark's LinkedIn Recommendation for Guy:
"My university research center concentrates on R&D in evidence–based performance improvement and one of our goals is to keep track of the activities of top professionals. Guy Wallace constantly appears on our radar as the best current example of the consummate professional in our field. His broad experience, constant creativity, successful work for his clients and his original contributions to our field all sum together into a very impressive career.

Guy has been working in the same field for a quarter century and he could easily rest on his past accomplishments. Yet he continues to create novel and exciting solutions for his clients. He invests considerable effort and so understands both best practice and the huge body of research and evaluation that supports practice.

He also spends quality time helping younger colleagues develop and works to advance our profession though professional organizations such as the International Society for Performance Improvement (where he was elected President a few years back) and the American Society for Training and Development.

But what impresses me most about Guy is his ability to think clearly about very complex problems. He has an exceptional talent for stepping back from complex issues and generating simple solutions and insights that are both sensible and effective."

– Dick Clark – June 27, 2009

The Curriculum Manager's Handbook

Guy W. Wallace

Details of Guy's background, accomplishments, education and experiences on over 250 client projects may be found at his web site at:

www.eppic.biz

Guy has been offering formal workshops and less formal coaching sessions on various analysis and design methods, as presented in this book, since 1984. His past clients for these awareness, knowledge and skills development efforts include: Amoco, AT&T, Dow Chemical, Discover Card, EDS, Eli Lilly, General Motors, HP, MCC Powers (later Siemens Building Technologies), the Norfolk Naval Shipyard, NAVSEA, NASCO, NCR, the NSA, and SunTrust.

The Wallace 6-Pack
for Instructional Systems Design for an Enterprise Context
- Paperback and Kindle -

1. The Curriculum Manager's Handbook
2. Analysis of Performance Competence Requirements
3. Performance-Based Curriculum Architecture Design
4. Performance-Based Modular Curriculum Development
5. Developing Your Management Areas of Performance Competence
6. From Training to Performance Improvement Consulting

- Guy W. Wallace Books For Sale *new in 2011* **-
See the Resources Tab at: www.eppic.biz**

Printed in Great Britain
by Amazon.co.uk, Ltd.,
Marston Gate.